S0-ARX-587

THE EDEN LEGACY
and the Decline of British Diplomacy

Also by Geoffrey McDermott
BERLIN: SUCCESS OF A MISSION?

THE EDEN LEGACY

and the

Decline of British Diplomacy

GEOFFREY McDERMOTT

LESLIE FREWIN : LONDON

© Geoffrey McDermott, 1969

First published in 1969 by Leslie Frewin Publishers Limited,
1 New Quebec Street, Marble Arch, London W1

Set in Baskerville
Printed by Anchor Press
and bound by William Brendon,
both of Tiptree, Essex

World Rights Reserved

09 096250 8

DA
566
.7
M26

Contents

Author's Note

I AM MOST grateful to Dennis Hackett and to my eldest son, Anthony McDermott, for their detailed and highly constructive comments on the first draft of this book. I have incorporated most of their suggestions and it is all the better for them.

GEOFFREY MCDERMOTT
January 1969

ONE

The Fatal Flaws

DIPLOMACY HAS NEVER been the strongest point of the British. Other gifts once made us the most powerful nation on earth: conquest, colonisation and trade, with 'trade following the flag'. The Italians, the French and in turn the Germans under Bismarck devoted more thought to the practice of effective diplomacy. Bismarck's concept of war as a legitimate extension of diplomacy, provided that the circumstances were carefully weighed, was a revolutionary and successful one. Its crude mishandling by later German governments has led to Germany's parlous state and division into three parts today.

The British story was different. While we added almost negligently to our empire up to the First World War our diplomats' main duties were to represent their sovereign, to keep relations good so that trade might flourish, and to prevent the rise of any overpowerful hostile alliance. This called for both an accurate assessment of power changes and a corresponding flexibility of our policy which earned us the title of 'perfidious Albion'. This is not a polite title, but it conceals some justified envy of our adaptability in the flux of international relations.

But when the long peaceful summer of the nineteenth century was shattered by the Bismarckian thunder we began to lose our diplomatic touch and judgment. The style remained the same: all too much so. The conditions, needs and aims of diplomacy began to change at an ever-increasing tempo, but our own adaptability gave place to more rigid attitudes. In the First World War we lost a generation and had to be rescued by the Americans. At the end of it we still had the empire; but the balance vis-à-vis the US and Japan was basically altered. Within a few years the empire, too, changed beyond recognition. The fatal flaw in our diplomacy was that it never kept up with these changes.

In that inter-war world it was less and less true that trade followed the Union Jack. In the first place the flag was not going places as before; and other flags were offering increasing competition. Secondly the United States was overtaking us in industrial and financial power. Thirdly our own economy was not developing as it should. Fourthly, although the first Labour governments came into power the social scene and hierarchy remained substantially conservative. In particular our diplomacy was entrusted, as it always had been, exclusively to the hands of the upper classes. This was just as much the case under the first two Labour Foreign Secretaries, Ramsay MacDonald and 'Uncle' Arthur Henderson, as the Foreign Office affectionately called him, as it was under the traditionalists. The great majority of the people were not interested in diplomacy and felt unable to understand it. They were happy to leave it to the experts.

What was required at this stage in our diplomacy was a new ingenuity and approach, and had they materialised they could have done much to mitigate our decline. But they did not appear. Marquesses, Earls and so on succeeded each other as Foreign Secretary. The Diplomatic Service and Foreign Office continued in the prewar style. Calmness, coolness and good manners continued to prevail. There were able men in the service, but they lacked the dynamism essential for coping with a dynamic age. Our diplomacy did little, if anything, to delay Britain's gentle slide downwards. The longer the slide continued, the more pronounced the effects became for Britain and for those of both her friends and enemies who realised what was developing.

I have linked my account of these crucial years with the name of Anthony Eden for a variety of reasons. There is no suggestion that our blundering diplomacy was all Eden's fault. It derived from our economic and social failures and from the profound conservatism and inertia of our diplomats and their set-up. Nevertheless, there was an Eden epoch. From the mid-twenties to the mid-fifties Eden more or less personified our diplomacy in the eyes of the British public and of the world, including both friend and foe. During nearly thirty years of crucial importance to Britain and the world he was on the diplomatic scene, usually in office – as a junior minister, then three times as Foreign Secretary, finally and most disastrously as Prime Minister – but also when in opposition. Moreover he left an account, eighteen hundred pages long, of his career and I have based my own account of the period largely on his testimony. Finally, I was in a position to observe events closely, and Eden's part in them, throughout most of the epoch. When I entered the Foreign Office in October 1935 he was Minister for League of Nations Affairs, and he became Foreign Secretary for the first time a couple of months later. And throughout the Suez crisis of 1956 which brought him down I was one of only three Foreign Office officials who were in on the political and strategic planning of the Suez campaign.

The legacy of the Eden style remained with us after he left the scene. I have tried, finally, to analyse its effects on the dozen years since then, during which I retired early from the Foreign Office and have been writing about diplomacy. In particular I have tried to suggest how we might make up for lost time, and remove the fatal flaws.

TWO

Full Circle

THE LAST YEARS of the Eden epoch were in a sense an epitome of the whole. In 1954 he was riding high. In his memoirs he lists a number of problems which he had helped to solve: the constitution of Western European Union; a new treaty with Egypt; a settlement in Indo-China; the restoration of good relations with Iran after the Abadan crisis; the agreement on the Buraimi oasis.

On the personal side, the Queen made him a Knight of the Garter. Even more gratifying, the aged and failing Winston Churchill, after changing his mind a dozen times over the years, at last decided to step down, and Eden became Prime Minister in April 1955.

From that moment on the curve went steadily down for him – steadily, that is, until it plunged to rock bottom over the Suez affair. In less than two years he was out of Number Ten and out of politics. A seemingly brilliant career crashed in flames.

The majority of the nation, who supported the Conservative Party at the time, were bewildered. They had liked Eden's elegance and respected him as the embodiment of all that a British diplomat should be. They were inclined to sympathise with him and consider him a tragic figure.

But people who knew him better and had worked closely with him could see matters in a truer light. The *débâcle,* or something like it, was predictable. Eden had set a style which practically all Foreign Office men followed, and so the tragedy involved was not just a personal one. It was a collapse of our traditional approach to foreign affairs as a whole. In his farewell speech on television in January 1957 Eden said that he was the same striver after peace, morality, justice and so on as he had been in the 1930s. This was all too true, but not in the way he meant it. Even in the 1930s his efforts had not achieved much, and after the Suez episode Britain's situation slid further down the scale. The world was moving on at a furious pace, but he, and British diplomacy in general, were not moving with it. One of his remarks was that modern communications corrupt good manners. This betrays a delusion that the admittedly 'good-mannered' diplomacy of earlier centuries was also smooth and gentle in its content. That was not the experience of those who had to deal with such as Bismarck, or with some of those Turkish Sultans who made a habit of dropping repugnant ambassadors down an *oubliette* into the Bosphorus; and the remark is no doubt intended to explain why a gentleman can hardly be expected to cope with diplomacy today. There is indeed something in that. For the cold fact is that most of today's diplomats have no wish to be or behave like British gentlemen. Most of them are not, after all, white. They are black, brown or yellow.

The principal aims of diplomacy are to win and keep friends and to influence people. When Eden first took office in 1931 Britain's situation was none too good, but she had influence as an imperial power and a few true friends. By the end of 1956 that power had vanished, Britain had been condemned in the world forum of the United Nations, and her actions had brought the US and the USSR into collaboration for the first time on record. The disasters of 1956 had far outweighed the 'successes' of 1954.

It would be absurd to hold Eden solely responsible for all this, but the flaw was there, clearly detectable to those who worked with him. When in December 1935 he had stepped up from being Minister for League of Nations Affairs to Foreign Secretary for his first brief spell we FO juniors were hopeful. Here was a man who had tried to make the peace-preserving machinery of the League of Nations work. I had been given Italy to handle at my low level, and I was flattered that from time to time the red ink which is the Foreign Secretary's prerogative was displayed in comments approving suggestions of mine for firmness in handling Mussolini. The trouble was that nothing came of it all. Mussolini outwitted Eden.

Over the years I could observe Eden, and the Eden-style FO, proceeding suavely along a steadily descending path in world affairs. When it came to 1956 Eden's progressive crack-up became more and more apparent. But no one in either Westminster or Whitehall was able, or willing, to stop the rot.

Churchill wrote: 'The use of recriminating about the past is to enforce effective action for the future.' It is in that spirit and hope that I have probed British diplomacy in the Eden era, and in the dozen years since. Excoriation as such is no part of my plan. It seemed right to base myself largely on his three volumes of memoirs, which are revealing in many ways, sometimes unwittingly. He seldom has a complimentary word to say about his colleagues, British or foreign. In return both British and foreign accounts of the period simply have rather little to say about Eden. George Kennan never mentions him. Lord Chandos mentions him about three times, and damns him with faint praise. He was 'not an easy man to know. His elegant appearance, disregard of men's clubs, appreciation of painting, liking of female society, perhaps concealed the inflexible nature of his principles on high matters of State. . . . Sometimes impatient and even petulant. . . . His sense of balance led him away from phrase-making, often as far as undistinguished language. . . . Until Suez he was always heard with attention and respect. . . . The Opposition, over Suez, fell far short of the standards which he himself had always set.'[1] So did Eden himself, as we shall see. Lord Moran relates that Churchill told Eden that to be a good House of Commons man he ought to spend an hour a day in the smoke-room there. Eden replied that he

[1] *Memoirs*, Viscount Chandos, Bodley Head, 1962.

supposed so, but he just didn't like it. Political colleagues and high officials and officers who collaborated closely with him have remarked on his almost feminine sensibility. He refers occasionally to his love of flowers, painting and poetry, and there is certainly no harm in that. But his entire intellectual, writing and speech-making style is the epitome of the middle-brow. I confess to a personal preference for the frankly high or low. Wittgenstein or Adam Diment, *si*; Galsworthy, no. Nor do I see why an admittedly important subject such as diplomacy should always be treated in a pompous and recondite manner rather than in words, sentences and thoughts which are intelligible to the ordinary reader.

Eden's memoirs have a further grave lack. In spite of their length they by no means tell the full story. Some of the official documents now becoming available show that various issues of the 1930s in which Eden was involved have been blurred in his account of them. The emphasis has been shifted from what was historically accurate. And in the volume covering Suez there is, to take the outstanding example from amongst various omissions, simply no mention of British collusion with Israel.

Balzac gives, in *Les Illusions Perdues,* a description of diplomacy which applies all too accurately to the story I have to tell. 'He considered himself a master of diplomacy, the science of those who possess no other and who are profound in their vacuity; a convenient science in that it fulfils itself merely in its exercise; a science which, requiring discretion, permits its practitioners to say nothing and shelter behind mysterious nods of the head; a science, finally, whose most successful exponent is he who can swim with his head above the stream of events he pretends to conduct; a science, in short, of specific levity.' Leaving aside any coincidental image of Chairman Mao floating down the Yangtse River, let us now survey British diplomacy proceeding at the decorous tempo of the breast-stroke, while the jets, the rockets and the thermonuclear weapons thunder above and below, around and about.

THREE

The Auspices

ROBERT ANTHONY EDEN was born in 1897 with every apparent advantage. His family was highly aristocratic – his father had the unusual distinction of being a baronet twice over, seventh in one line and fifth in another – and the family seat had been with them for three hundred years. They were well-off by all ordinary standards though Anthony would remark later on that he had never been a rich man.

He was sent to Eton. Amongst his contemporaries there were Harold Macmillan (three years older than he), the present Marquess of Salisbury, Viscount Chandos, Lord Boothby and literally scores of others who made a mark in politics. A large proportion of our top diplomats came from the same source. In the wider sphere he was in the same age group as Goering, Dean Acheson, Khrushchev, Robert Menzies, Bulganin, Oswald Mosley, Aneurin Bevan, Noël Coward, Paul Spaak, Mao Tse-tung, Chou En-lai, Presidents Kenyatta and Tubman, Emperor Hirohito, Chairman Ulbricht, the Pope, Earl Mountbatten and the Duke of Windsor, to take a fairly random selection.

At Eton he achieved nothing special. He fought bravely in the First World War and was awarded the Military Cross. He derived a curious illusion from his military service which he mentions several times in his memoirs. This was that there existed some sort of universal honour amongst soldiers which could be projected into the field of international relations. The Old Etonian major tried this one on both Hitler and Stalin, who were, to say the least, men of a rather different stamp. They can only have concluded that it represented some harmless English eccentricity. On the other hand Eden found it very difficult to establish normal relations with men such as Hugh Gaitskell, who had never had occasion to put on uniform. His comments on the various units that he visited in the Second World War are always cast in the traditional mould: they are 'a splendid body of men', 'first-class chaps' and so on.

He went to Christ Church, Oxford, after the war and came down with first-class honours in Oriental languages – Persian and Arabic – in 1922. When Churchill first heard of this some twenty years later he expressed astonishment rather than total admiration. The achievement was in fact untypical of Eden. He did not work by way of intellectual brilliance. Indeed, how many politicians do? Eden's work was particularly methodical, almost bureaucratic, until his latter days when ill-health and frustration taxed his patience and judgment. Similarly, while some of his earlier speeches had a certain freshness and drive he was no orator. In later years the expression and delivery became depressingly flat.

Eden was not politically active at Oxford but the political career seemed eminently suitable for one in his station in life and he went straight into it. He contested Spennymoor the moment he came down in 1922, unsuccessfully. The next year he won Warwick and Leamington and he remained their member until he retired in 1957. Also in 1923 he married a rich woman, Miss Beatrice Beckett. Without delay he was in 1925 appointed Parliamentary Private Secretary to G Locker-Lampson, Under-Secretary at the Home Office. In 1926 he got his foot on the Foreign Affairs ladder when he became PPS to the Foreign Secretary, Sir Austen Chamberlain. From then until his collapse thirty years later all his energies were devoted to diplomacy, though for a few months in 1940 he was at the War Office.

All the auspices, then, were excellent, and no career which ends up at Number Ten can be called a failure . . . and yet, and yet . . . what went wrong? I think the case can be analysed like this. The beginnings – with the exception of the First World War – were too easy. Everything fell into the lap of this handsome, gifted young member of what seemed a divinely appointed ruling class. Consorting only with his peers, he found it difficult to grasp the significance of socialism even though Labour came to power. Imagination was never a strong point of Eden's. As a result his efforts to get across to the poorer people tended to sound either stuffy or condescending. He often referred jocularly to his ignorance of economic affairs and he was unable to remedy this. He had none of the knockabout common sense that could make his contemporary Macmillan a first-class Minister of Housing or Chandos an excellent President of the Board of Trade, and both of them successful businessmen. Eden went at foreign affairs exclusively. Since Britain, out of all the major powers, depends on trade and a soundly organised economic base, and always has and will, this operating in the diplomatic void was bound to end in tears.

Eden began his climb to power at the very moment when the interaction of economic and political forces was about to take a brutal turn in the United States, across Europe and in the Far East. It was a testing time for traditional British diplomacy, and it failed the test.

The Decline Sharpens

IN 1929 WALL STREET crashed and for a second time, and in a different place, there were ten days that shook the world. The newly elected Labour government proved unable to cope with the consequences and was followed in 1931 by a National government with the tired Ramsay MacDonald still its titular head. One of the government's first actions was, unavoidably, to devalue the pound. In return we received loans from the US and France.

There were similar repercussions all over Europe. In Germany, in particular, the existing economic chaos became even worse. As a direct result the Nazis won a hundred and seven votes in the Reichstag elections of September 1930.

Also in 1929 Eden made the light-hearted comment: 'I, personally, am prepared to plead guilty to the charge of being merely an opportunist in these fiscal matters.'

He was by no means alone in this. The attitude was shared by all members of the FO and Diplomatic Service. Though a few consuls and such had an amateurish smattering of commercial affairs it was generally considered no part of a diplomat's business to know about trade and economic matters either at home or abroad. It was infra dig. Broad political ideas elegantly presented were the thing. To a considerable extent the attitude is still the same today.

The lesson that our diplomats should have drawn from the overwhelming effects of the Wall Street crash was that Britain, and the rest of the world, were far more dependent on the US than they had ever imagined. I have found that the typical British diplomat's attitude to the US, then as now, is complex and ambivalent. Almost all say that they are pro-American and find it easy to get on with Americans. Eden repeatedly said this. Then in confidence they will add that they find many Americans brash, embarrassingly rich, naive in diplomatic matters, a bit uncultivated. They are shocked if they are told in return that many American diplomats consider ours stuffy, embarrassingly poor, frighteningly traditional, sometimes wet. Not that many Americans say such things often; they are too considerate for that. If only these matters had been sorted out earlier on many of the Anglo-US misunderstandings of the Roosevelt era – and he was elected in 1932 also as an indirect result of the financial crash – might have been avoided.

What was needed on our side was a realistic assessment of the relative power of Britain and the US. As again after the Second World War the situation was deceptive. We had in fact been gently slipping in the economic contest since the 1870s. That is to say that, although our people as a whole were better off in the 1930s than in the 1870s, the standard of living of the US had risen much faster and had overtaken ours. Nevertheless we were still the great imperial power, and we reckoned to exert decisive influence in Europe as well. Our diplomats looked with some envy at their upstart American 'cousins' and criticised them – unjustifiably – for not wanting to help Europe. Instead of adopting a condescending attitude we would have done better to bring the Americans close to us by treating them as equals and acknowledging their growing power and influence. But, typically, for nine long and crucial years from 1930 to 1939 our ambassador in Washington was Sir Ronald Lindsay, a complete epitome of Victorian diplomacy.

The major fault in all this was on the part of the FO. But people get the sort of FO they deserve. It was completely accepted by the public in those days, and to a great extent is now, that diplomacy is an arcane pursuit which only gentlemen can master. Further, diplomacy is expected to be traditional in its content and tempo. Lord Chandos reports a revealing, if revolting, incident in the House of Commons: 'John McGovern, the Clydesider and a friend of mine, once said to me in the smoking-room: "Anthony is our idea of a gentleman. We respect him, but we shan't ever match him".' I often hear similar sentiments expressed in Worcestershire today. And look at the public furore when Bevin was appointed Foreign Secretary – until, that is, it was made clear that the FO had tamed him – and the well-bred sniffing at George Brown. With this permanent public backing our gentlemanly diplomats have gone serenely ahead, frequently offending other nations by their assumption of effortless superiority and frequently being caught short by more modern-minded and aggressive diplomacy. In the 1930s I was able to observe many lamentable examples.

In 1931 Eden was given by his mentor Stanley Baldwin the post of Under-Secretary at the FO, pipping Duff Cooper at the post. The job was far more important then than now. Not only was he the number two of only two FO ministers, where today the post ranks bottom of seven, but as the Foreign Secretary was, briefly, the Marquess of Reading, Eden was for a glorious two months the FO spokesman in the Commons. This was remedied in November 1931, however, when Sir John Simon became Foreign Secretary.

Eden's memoirs reveal early on, and with some candour throughout, a lasting characteristic of his. He was an uncomfortable colleague, both to his fellow-ministers and diplomats and to the foreigners with whom it was his business to collaborate. For instance he is highly critical throughout of his chiefs Sir John Simon and Neville Chamberlain. Unfortunately he also took against Sir Robert Vansittart who had become Permanent Under-Secretary of the FO in 1930 at the astonishingly early age – for the FO – of forty-eight. I was not alone in admiring Van warmly. To my mind he was the outstanding diplomat of the last generation. Even his handsomeness was of an original mould: he was *un joli laid*. His brain worked at about twice the normal speed. He could write not only powerful official papers but good poetry. He was most kind to his juniors. I remember to this day the grand, but not too grand, lunch to which he invited me immediately after I joined the FO, and how gently he dissuaded me from stirring my first ever cup of Turkish coffee. (Why, I have since reflected, was there a spoon?) Above all he kept up with the times and actually looked ahead of them. He immediately recognised the menace of Nazism and pounded home his warnings in a series of masterly memoranda on 'the old Adam' and 'the butcher bird'. He was not fettered by bureaucratic shackles. He had his private secret service in Germany. Quite unconstitutionally, but how profitably for the nation, he kept the government's chief opponent, Winston Churchill, fully briefed on the dangers.

The older Etonian's temperament was bound to clash with that of his younger minister. First, it irked Eden that in the FO hierarchy he ranked, as Parliamentary Under-Secretary, below Vansittart. But even when Eden was elevated the conflict continued. It was basic to policy; for where Eden broadly went along with his colleagues' 'appeasement', Van never did. On the personal side Van's style was more that of a Secretary of State, while Eden's methodical procedure caused a political colleague to comment that he could have stepped down to be Permanent Under-Secretary. So Van's warnings were not heeded and eventually Eden personally ousted him, kicking him upstairs to the otiose post, invented for the purpose, of Chief Diplomatic Adviser. Eden's own account of the operation is, as we shall see, highly disingenuous.

In Eden's dealings with foreign colleagues the same characteristics exhibit themselves. The awkwardness culminated in his complete alienation of his faithful French allies over Suez, not to mention the fact that he was at daggers drawn with Foster Dulles from the word go.

Curiously for a man who devoted his life to diplomacy Eden did not really like or understand foreigners. Quite a number of members of the FO are in the same case. The present number two in the FO has had a minimal number of posts away from Whitehall. Another senior official recently begged that he should not be promoted and transferred because 'he didn't like abroad'. As for Eden, someone who knew him well said that while he had no enemies he also had few friends. Alas, the first part of the statement is untrue.

The so-called National government stumbled on under Ramsay MacDonald from 1931 to 1935. It gave no great inspiration to the country and had little impact abroad. In the same period Hitler achieved total power when he became Chancellor in 1933. Few people apart from Churchill and Vansittart were prepared to do anything about the Nazis. At that stage there were two distinct possibilities of holding them in check. One was for Britain and France to get closer together with both the US and the USSR. The other was to play off Mussolini against Hitler over Austria. Neither was achieved.

Instead, Eden and the FO carried on the policies of the 1920s in the spirit of Locarno, to which Eden so often refers. (He did so even in 1956 in connexion with Suez.) In 1932 Eden was advocating, at the endless Disarmament Conference, the total abolition of military and naval aircraft. This is the type of suggestion which the Soviet government frequently put up in the late 1940s and the 1950s, knowing it to be wholly impracticable and then making the feeble propaganda point that the Western powers had rejected it. In addition MacDonald and Eden sponsored a draft convention complete in all details and asked the sixty members of the conference to swallow it whole. This had the result that might have been foreseen. The other members wondered whether Britain was making monkeys of them. Germany quit the conference in 1932. She was rearming fast in any case and had begun research on rockets in 1930. 'The solemn and prolonged farce', as Churchill called it, dragged on until it collapsed in 1934. Eden rejected his criticism of it, displaying a lasting characteristic of his own and of his fellow diplomats: so long as pieces of paper were being circulated, minutes written, drafts discussed and so on, diplomacy was being carried forward. The trouble was that for many countries the draft proposals were not worth the paper they were written on. More than that, they provided a handy time-wasting exercise for the aggressive nations who could get on with their military preparations while talking away at the conference table. Eden's spirit was quite different from that embodied in Churchill's well-known apophthegm that it is better to jaw, jaw than war, war. He, MacDonald and the FO really believed that diplomatic propositions, however impracticable, had a sort of life and virtue of their own. And meanwhile the defences of Britain were being improved at only a snail's pace.

Since British diplomacy in the 1930s was imbued with this spirit it is not surprising that it staggered on from failure to failure, or that such successes as it achieved were either small, temporary or counterproductive. In March 1933 Churchill roundly attacked MacDonald's foreign affairs activities as having 'brought us nearer war than ever before'. Eden defended him and Ramsay toyed with the idea of awarding him a KCB, normally given to civil servants in their fifties. He was actually promoted Lord Privy Seal and, in 1934, Privy Councillor, though without a seat in the Cabinet as yet. All this time Eden was slogging away at the League of Nations as if that moribund body could achieve something. But Germany flounced out in 1933. Vansittart proposed that she should be formally arraigned before the League; but Eden squashed the proposal and does not even mention it in his memoirs. As early as 1933 Vansittart commented on the League's increasing disrepute, while Eden continued for years to trust its efficacity against all the evidence. By January 1934 Sir Eric Phipps, an old-style ambassador but with sharp powers of observation, forecast in his despatches from Berlin that the Nazis were likely to go to war within a few years. Phipps had an admirably dry style, as when reporting one of Hitler's rodomontades he inserted the comment: 'here I smiled'. Again, Hitler's proposition that the SA (*Sturm Abteilungen*, or Storm Troops) were a similar body to our own SA, or Salvation Army, was not calculated to convince him. He was never taken in by the Nazis and reported fearlessly on them. Of course they did not love him for it. On Eden's orders he was replaced by the pro-Nazi Sir Nevile Henderson in 1937. Henderson requited this favour by showing open jubilation when Eden was removed from the Foreign Secretaryship in 1938.

The US had expressed sympathy with the principles underlying the British disarmament suggestions of 1932, but according to Eden they made it clear that they were not in any way participants in European problems, and he comments that while they called for disarmament they contributed the least to security. Although the US's non-participation in the League was to be deplored Eden's remarks show a misunderstanding of the US attitude. He and the FO never tried hard enough to bring the US in. Eden refers infrequently to them and always critically. He never bothered to visit the US while in power. His first visit was a brief one in December 1938; he was summoned to his next one five years later by President Roosevelt.

Typical of the diplomatic pseudo-successes of those years was a splendid declaration in December 1932 by Britain, France, Germany and Italy renouncing the use of force in settling differences. The immediate result was Germany's return to the Disarmament Conference – for just ten months. As for the longer-term effects, no comment seems necessary. The Rome Pact of 1933 confirmed the adherence of the same four powers to the League Covenant, the Locarno treaties and the Kellogg-Briand Pact. The two dictators must have fallen about laughing up their sleeves. In fact relations between them were not perfect at this time, as a meeting in Venice in June 1934 showed. But our policy continued to be based on waffling about the League and collective security rather than on exploiting the differences between the two.

MacDonald, Simon and Eden continued their series of visits to Geneva and the capitals of Europe, with little to show for it. On one tour including Berlin in 1934 Eden comments that his colleagues in the Cabinet showed a lack of confidence in his handling and that he received what amounted to a rebuke. He criticised the French government for not backing him up and, in schoolmasterly fashion, for 'not doing their homework'.

On the question of relations with the Soviet Union Eden showed some enterprise and originality. One of the new Labour government's first actions in 1929 had been to restore relations with the USSR: these had been broken thanks to the Tory exploitation of the forged 'Zinoviev letter' in 1924. Similarly President Roosevelt 'recognised' the USSR in 1933. In 1934, mainly owing to efforts by the French for which Eden gives them due credit, the Soviet Union was actually admitted to the League of Nations. The power which within a few years was to be the second super-power in the world was granted the privilege of collaborating with that useless and teetering organisation. The Soviet government was realistic enough to accept this as a useful opportunity of increasing its contacts with all sorts of nations. Eden for his part was realistic enough to understand that the French government viewed the move as a possible counter to Germany's increasing military power. But, he remarks sadly, this policy was not popular with some of his Cabinet colleagues 'and particularly the older ones, who were less realistic'.

He was not realistic on all questions himself. He ventured the assertion that by the end of 1934 Britain's authority and the League's stood higher than ever before. However in early 1935 he went on a trip to Berlin and Moscow which should have been worthwhile. From Berlin he sent a gloomy report to London on which Vansittart minuted: 'These views seem very sound'. But the Cabinet did not agree.

Eden then became the first British minister to visit the Soviet Union since the revolution, and the first Western political representative to be received by Stalin. Of course his approach was that all Communists, and particularly their leaders, were savages. So it is not surprising if his comments are condescending on the whole. He noticed that Stalin always appeared well laundered and neatly dressed; well, for a man who, like royalty, never had to handle money, this is not too surprising. But Eden even admitted to 'a sympathy which I have never been able to analyse'. He could not believe that Stalin 'had any affinity with Marx'. Stalin showed what the youngish Eden considered 'a remarkable knowledge and understanding of international affairs'. We may today reflect that the meetings at Tehran, Yalta and Potsdam were not all that far off. Morosely, Eden wondered what his colleagues' reaction to his talks with Stalin would be: 'Unenthusiastic, I felt sure'.

Equally morosely on the personal front his reflexion on one colleague's comment that younger men such as he should take over was: 'I was to get used to hearing it in the next twenty-one years.' And his minuting style had not tightened up. One long minute which he considered important contained all the following gems: 'Personally, I have for some time past been anxious about the drift of events. . . . It is hard to believe that. . . . It would seem now that Italy aims at no less than . . . In this connexion it is perhaps not without interest to note that. . . . I venture to think that it must be a matter of serious concern to us. . . . The impression that is left on my mind by all this is that unless. . . . It is surely at least possible that. . . .' It is easy to see that Churchill's comment on one of his wartime memos was justified: that it contained all the clichés except 'please adjust your dress before leaving'.[1]

By the end of 1934 it did indeed 'seem that Italy aims at no less than' the conquest of Abyssinia. In February 1935 she sent troops to East Africa and there could be no further

[1] *Memoirs*, Earl of Avon, Cassell, 1960–5.

doubt of her intentions. A last effort in April 1935 to get agreement between Britain, France and Italy against the greater menace of Nazi expansionism, which at least the French recognised, hardly got off the ground. In June Stanley Baldwin took over the National Government, though MacDonald still tagged along, and Eden hoped that his friend would give him the FO. But influential people like Neville Chamberlain and Geoffrey Dawson of *The Times* made their opposition clear and once more Eden was disappointed. Sir Samuel Hoare, one of the real old-fashioned gang, got the job. However Eden received a seat in the Cabinet with the specially contrived post of Minister for League of Nations Affairs. It could have been foreseen that two Cabinet ministers of such different temperament would hardly work in harness inside the FO. So it proved. Moreover Eden was immediately allocated the impossible task of appeasing Mussolini. Not that Abyssinia's rights were to be respected; but he was to offer Mussolini certain concessions on condition that the dictator acted in accordance with the Covenant of the League. Not only did the attempt fail, but Eden and Mussolini conceived a personal antagonism for each other – though Eden attempts to blur this in his account – which was to contribute much to Eden's fall in 1938.

Eden's account of the next few months is a list of his failures. He was all for locking the stable door now that the horse had bolted; but his colleagues would not even have that. He wanted to tell Laval that HMG would fulfil all her obligations under the Covenant: 'Not approved by my colleagues'. On raising the arms embargo in favour of Abyssinia he argued for weeks with Hoare and, he says, Vansittart; he wrote copious minutes; but he failed, as 'might be expected with two Cabinet ministers in the FO'. 'London curbs me again' is the title of a chapter. He was told that he was over-enthusiastic about sanctions, and of course he was. His ignorance of economic matters showed itself again here. When Italy invaded Abyssinia in October 1935 the League imposed sanctions. It had to. Then it could rub its hands and declare its duty done. The only flaw was that they had no effect. As soon as Italy had overrun and annexed Abyssinia in May 1936 the same League representatives, including Eden, had to get together and raise sanctions, which they hastily did in July 1936. By then Mussolini was locked in a fond embrace with Hitler, who had not opposed him; and the League of Nations was a dead duck. The policy of HMG, as carried out by Hoare and Eden, had contributed substantially to these catastrophic results.

However, in December 1935 Hoare had gone off on a skating holiday and fallen through the thin ice. It is well known how he called on Laval in Paris and produced the notorious Hoare-Laval proposals which in effect congratulated Mussolini and confirmed that he must keep the fruits of his aggression. Eden notes that this was Hoare's first meeting with Laval at which he himself was not present. What a bit of luck for Eden! He considered resigning. Instead, he did just the opposite. As HMG's spokesman he pressed fellow-members of the League to urge the Emperor of Abyssinia to accept the terms. He failed again in this. Even the lethargic British public could not stand such a capitulation. The US government indicated its displeasure. Hoare had to resign on 18th December. Of course he was given high office again after a decent interval and made a Viscount.

Even now Eden's succession was not certain. Baldwin toyed with the idea of Austen Chamberlain, who was by now unfortunately gaga, and Halifax. The powerful elders in the Cabinet did not care for Eden. It is difficult to see why not. He had gone faithfully along with their policy of appeasement. He had shared fully in the series of failures which it had achieved. He had shown throughout his great respect for Baldwin, and finally a combination of these considerations did the trick. At the age of thirty-eight, which seemed madly young *dans cette galère* even if we should consider it today as the onset of middle age, Anthony Eden had

31

his heart's desire. On 18th December 1935 he became Foreign Secretary for the first time. The *New Statesman* facetiously described the appointment as 'Mr Baldwin's Christmas present to the nation'.

FIVE

The Slippery Slope

MY WORM'S-EYE view enabled me to see some features of the FO scene for which a harassed new Foreign Secretary could hardly have time – the characters of my fellow-beginners in October 1935, for instance. With one exception we were much the same mixture as usual. Of the two who have done best in their careers one actually failed the exam and came in later by the side door; the next came bottom. They are both Etonians with titles. Of the remaining six only two are still in the service, inching their way towards honourable retirement. I myself came from a family with no money and no diplomatic connexions at all. I was urged in that direction by a schoolmaster on the grounds that my languages were good. He cannot have heard some of our distinguished envoys massacring French or jibbing at German. The exceptional one was Donald Maclean, son of the Liberal Cabinet minister, and everyone knows that he has been operating in the Soviet Union since 1951 after spying most efficiently on that country's behalf while in the British Embassy in Washington and elsewhere. He did particularly well in the interview part of the examination thanks to his suave deportment, his 'typically British' appearance and his general charm.

The fact that the three notorious traitors Philby, Maclean and Burgess all made up their minds to serve Communism in the early 1930s is no coincidence. I was at Cambridge with all of them though I only met them, sporadically, later on. Intelligent and politically minded undergraduates looked around at successive British governments and their foreign policies and did not at all like what they saw. The capitalist system appeared to be cracking up and offering little but a prolonged depression. Many students all over Britain agreed with the Oxford Union resolution of February 1933 that they would 'in no circumstances fight for King and Country'. The Tories bumbled hypocritically and ineffectually along, their leading group clinging to the power which they considered to be theirs by right and getting steadily further behind events in the process. They stuck firmly to the delusion that the dictators could be made to see reason by means of old-fashioned diplomacy. The Socialists smashed themselves in two in 1931 and were neither inspiring nor effectual. The only people who seemed to take the repeated aggressions of the Nazis and Fascists seriously were the Communists. They foresaw that war would come and they took measures wherever they could to ensure that Soviet Communism, a New Civilisation (as Sidney and Beatrice Webb justifiably called it), should emerge from that war stronger, and the rest of Europe weaker. As Philby put it, 'knowing what I knew I could act in no other way'.

These traitors' way was made smooth by the facts that they belonged to the 'right' class and that their fellows simply could not conceive that they would do the 'wrong' thing. Thus while both Maclean and Philby were spying brilliantly for the Soviet Union they were also achieving brilliant careers in the FO and the Secret Intelligence Service. Even when Maclean and Burgess had defected in 1951 many of their colleagues refused to believe it was true. The strong evidence that Philby was the third man who had tipped them off just in time was not accepted by his peers. He continued to do some work for the SIS and defected at leisure in 1963. People like these, in the positions which they occupied in the forties and fifties, were able to affect British and American diplomacy and policy to a grave extent. Maclean passed to the Russians a number of American nuclear secrets which significantly shortened the time in which they achieved nuclear parity. Philby enabled

34

the Communists to wreck the CIA-SIS operation in Albania in 1950 which could, if successful, have stirred up the Balkans against their Communist overlords. He also kept them informed of the deployment of our, and most of the CIA's, secret agents world-wide. And the whole time the traitors were subtly angling their reports and decisions so as to render nugatory a good deal of the West's diplomacy.

I was a more naive character than these. I was aware of the pro-Communist circles at Cambridge and could see the logic of some of their arguments. I was never tempted to join them but I went so far as to read some of their source books such as Marx and Mehring in the original. For the sake of knowing our main enemy's mind I also worked through the turgid *Mein Kampf*. It has always seemed to me of the first importance to study the mentality and methods of your opponents – and your friends – so that your decisions and actions are not taken in the void or merely in accordance with some general, established principles. This attitude probably accounted for such success as I later had when Foreign Office Adviser to the Chief of the Secret Service. But the Foreign Office, with few exceptions, preferred the traditional methods and were suspicious of intelligence. Most diplomats were doubtful whether it was either reliable or gentlemanly. Many, particularly amongst our senior ambassadors today, still hold similar views. Eden, Macmillan and Douglas-Home always treated it lightly.

Consequently in the 1930s few members of the Foreign Office had any inkling of the ferment outside its walls. The atmosphere was leisurely; we were a family, on Christian-name terms. It was the old boy net *in excelsis*.

Work began at 11 am, in order to allow the messenger on the Channel packet time to reach London by post-chaise from Dover, according to the then current joke. Two hours were allowed for lunch, few people worked after six in the afternoon, and it was understood that anyone invited to a tennis party would leave at five in summer. Van himself was no great believer in the merits of mountains of paper-work as such, and I based myself on his good example. True, however, one new entrant went a bit far and was refused permission to take three days off each week during the hunting season. The long weekend was taken for granted, and it was considered not cricket when the dictators regularly executed their coups during that sacrosanct period. The resident clerks in the FO were not asked to curtail their social activities. On the contrary, they were considered to be doing their duty fully in any emergency if they left with the switchboard the telephone number of the house where they were dining or the theatre where they were amusing themselves. I was a resident clerk for a while and much enjoyed life on my handsome salary of about £300 a year. I think I rather alarmed some of my more conventional colleagues by displaying the surrealist pictures and objects which were to my taste. Meanwhile, of course, a large number of very tough diplomats of quite a different stamp were busy night and day in Berlin, Rome, Tokyo and Moscow. These were men who considered diplomacy too important to be left to the professional diplomats; and who saw in war a practical extension of diplomacy.

But it was all most enjoyable on the inside. I was chosen by Owen O'Malley to work in his Southern Department because he liked my Irish name. The size varied from four to six members at different times and we dealt with the whole of southern Europe including Italy. As the most junior person handling that country it fell to me to 'minute' all relevant papers first, and the fruits of my mature wisdom were then propelled up the hierarchy at a moderate pace, reaching the Secretary of State himself when the particular paper was of sufficient importance. That was how it had always been, and was going to continue. It is not surprising that our diplomacy was inadequate. The Foreign Office's contacts with other government departments were both loose and condescending. The Dominions and Colonial Offices, who after all dealt with large and important parts of the world, were regarded almost as lesser breeds without the law.

Co-ordination of policy with economic and military departments was haphazard and largely on a personal basis. There was no forward planning such as I encouraged twenty years later when I was head of the Permanent Under-Secretary's Department, a central department for overall politico-military strategy which did not exist in the thirties. Neither Eden nor Vansittart, much though he was to be admired politically, made any effort to speed up the system. It took a war and Churchill to do that.

One extra-curricular duty that fell to me turned out most agreeably. On the death of George V in January 1936 notables from all over the world flocked to London. The FO were asked to produce, amongst others, a German interpreter and I was chosen. I walked over to Number Ten with trepidation which was soon lulled by a very friendly welcome from Baldwin's Principal Private Secretary, Sir Geoffrey Fry. He explained to me that Baldwin had stoutly averred that he would rather take down his trousers in public than speak a word of any foreign language. In the upshot my services were not required because the foreign envoys had no such inhibitions about speaking English. I rather regretted this; I should have enjoyed watching Baldwin cope with all those funny foreigners, as he considered them. A curious piece of diplomacy. My own reward was a long and warm friendship with Geoffrey Fry.

When he looked back on those days Eden made clear his dislike of Vansittart. After praising his many virtues he adds that his language was sometimes obscure and tortured. While his instinct was usually right his political methods were at fault. Here Eden was correct; for thanks to his *excès de zèle* Van in fact failed to get his case across. Ignorant as I was of the domestic politics and personal conflicts involved this seemed both strange and regrettable to me. For Van's case was simply that we should build up all possible strength in Europe, and beyond, to curb Hitler. Eden did not care for his 'repetitive fervour'. Above all, he was, in fact, right. That was unpardonable.

37

The clash of views became clear without delay. Early in 1936 Eden wrote in a minute: 'We should make concessions to Germany, and concessions of value to her, but only as part of a final settlement which includes some further [sic] arms limitation and Germany's return to the League.' It was the usual trouble: these ideas appeared to make sense but happened to be wholly unrealistic and impracticable. Eden continued to pay too much attention to the weaker dictator and consequently not enough to the stronger. Vansittart would have liked to play it the other way round.

We young officials, ignorant of the political in-fighting that was going on, had high hopes of Eden as Foreign Secretary. The black homburg known as the Anthony Eden hat became part of our uniform. His handsome head, bland manner and natty dressing were much admired. But what we did not realise was that he never had a chance of operating with the full powers and prestige of a Foreign Secretary. The old gang in the Cabinet had overruled him often enough before; they continued to do so now. There were three senior ex-Foreign Secretaries for a start – MacDonald (admittedly gaga by now), Simon and Hoare. Baldwin took only a fitful interest in foreign affairs. He left his protégé Eden to get on with it as best he could. For his part Eden faithfully maintained that Baldwin was the only statesman we had.

During Eden's first year in office the international scene deteriorated at an alarming pace. He and Flandin, the new French Foreign Minister, contrived in January 1936 to reach the conclusion that the Fascist position was weakening, and in February Eden recommended that the two countries should negotiate 'betimes' with Hitler about the Rhineland demilitarised zone. Too late. Hitler seized it in March. Now Eden began to doubt his good faith. He applauded the view of the French and Belgian governments that Hitler must be pulled up now or it might never be possible. But whereas Flandin roundly declared: 'If you do not stop Germany today, war is inevitable,' Eden and his colleagues drew the conclusion that a far-reaching settlement must, and could, now be reached with Hitler. Ribbentrop told Eden that if Anglo-French staff talks were held further negotiations with Hitler would be impossible. He recorded smugly: 'Happily Mr Eden did not make things more difficult for me.' Indeed he did not. He accepted the German government's comments on their action as showing Germany's 'unchangeable longing for a real pacification of Europe'. It depends, of course, on what you mean by pacification: 'They make a desert, and call it peace'. But Eden went on about 'collective security', which A J P Taylor calls a 'fifth wheel of British policy, added for ostentation, not use', while at last beginning to have doubts about the League's efficacy. None too soon: as he sadly comments Germany, Japan and the US were outside it, Mussolini was breaking the Covenant, and the USSR was 'unpredictable'. He remarked during a Cabinet discussion that he was not prepared to be the first Foreign Secretary to go back on a British signature. With all his innumerable worries he could have spared himself that one. Albion had a well-established reputation for perfidy, acquired in the nineteenth and early twentieth centuries when we exploited the trait to good effect in maintaining the balance of power in Europe. What is pathetic is to see how our diplomacy in the 1930s wavered and changed course frequently but without achieving any solid effects. It was frustrating for us officials who could only keep on putting up our bright ideas and do what we were told when they were turned down.

May and June 1936 were rough. In May Mussolini formally annexed Abyssinia. In England there was mounting pressure to lift sanctions, partly because it was thought that the navy deserved some leave from its not very arduous patrol duties in the Mediterranean. In June Neville Chamberlain, then Chancellor of the Exchequer and in Eden's view 'such a steadfast colleague', denounced sanctions as 'the very midsummer of madness'. He wrote in his diary: 'I did it deliberately. . . . I felt the country needed a lead. . . . I did not consult Eden about it. . . . He has been as nice as possible about it though he has had to suffer in the public interest.' So Eden, who had backed sanctions with such enthusiasm, had to propose their ending, which was effected in July. He comments that he did not feel called upon to resign 'for I had not had control of policy'. A sad admission for a Foreign Secretary.

Just one hopeful development occurred in these months. In France the Popular Front, including the Communists, won a resounding electoral victory and came to power under Léon Blum, a Socialist. Here was a real hope of bringing the USSR actively in on the preservation of peace through a firm attitude to the dictators. But Eden, who had not got on well with the right-wing Flandin, of course could not get on terms with his left-wing successor Blum. This kindly Jew, who was about as much of a firebrand as Attlee, was regarded by the high Tories as tarred with the Communist brush. And so the alliance stumbled on.

It stumbled, for example, into the non-policy of non-intervention in the Spanish civil war which broke out in July. It is a fact that in diplomacy you must sometimes talk nonsense. It is essential that when you do so you are aware that you are doing so; fatal if you deceive yourself. When the Spanish ambassador told Eden as early as September 1936 that non-intervention would militate against the Spanish government Eden told him stiffly that non-intervention was his policy and he would not modify it. Yet it was perfectly clear to large numbers of people in Britain and elsewhere that the ambassador was right. Hundreds of young British volunteers rushed to Spain to fight for the government and remedy the official non-intervention by their personal intervention against the new dictator. I read with enthusiasm the poems, stories and reports produced by the numerous talented writers amongst them. Philby however went as a journalist to Franco's side, to spy for his Soviet masters. He was very nearly killed by a Communist shell and received a decoration from Franco. Eden's policy over Abyssinia had been to refuse help to the country's established government. It was

40

the same with Spain now. Both failed disastrously. He refused a Labour demand that arms should be sent to the Spanish government not because he was not aware that the dictators were sending them to Franco but because 'the evidence we had at this time against the Russians was more specific'. In October he said: 'Non-intervention is a device [*sic*] by means of which we hope to limit the risks of total war in Spain and a European war out of that'. Failure, once again, all along the line: Guernica and the other horrors in Spain, the Second World War following hot on the Spanish civil war.

In November 1936 Mussolini took several interlocking diplomatic initiatives. He proclaimed the existence of the Rome-Berlin axis. And he indicated that he would like what Eden, perhaps for subconscious reasons, repeatedly miscalls 'a gentleman's agreement' with Britain. The point is that it takes two gents, in the plural, to make that sort of agreement. Mussolini's effrontery paid off. Eden, while protesting unconvincingly that he had no personal vendetta' against Mussolini, thought to prove it by instructing HM ambassador in Rome, Sir Eric Drummond, to negotiate the agreement. It was hustled through and published on 2nd January 1937. One of its avowed objects was to maintain the independence of Spain. Count Ciano had insisted on excluding France, and Eden acquiesced. This was yet another agreement that was not worth the paper it was written on. Even at the time Eden had no doubt that the increased Fascist intervention in Spain 'was a violation of the spirit of the Agreement', especially as that intervention had gone so far as the recognition in November 1936 of Franco's government by both Hitler and Mussolini. Never mind; according to the traditional diplomatic principles something had been achieved because a sheet of paper headed 'Agreement' had been signed and delivered. I found it all most disturbing.

Eden now proposed that some sort of watch on non-intervention – or rather, intervention – should be instituted. Not only was it far too late; but Hoare, now at the Admiralty, and the rest of the Cabinet rejected the plan as too anti-Franco. Laughably, the actual protocol on non-intervention was signed in London only in December 1936. Eden himself, 'if he had to choose', would have preferred a government victory, he says. It was safe to say this; he was not in a position to choose. When the opposition taunted the government with its favouritism to Fascism and tyranny Eden's comment was: 'The Labour Party has always had its share of vicarious warriors.' This was at a moment when some of its active warriors were laying down their lives in Spain.

In a speech which he chooses to quote in his memoirs, made in the House on 19th January 1937 Eden referred to the desire of the peoples of the world for peace. This is an example of loose thinking positively dangerous in diplomacy. The peoples of Germany, Italy and Japan did not desire peace; they wanted war. 'Our objective must be the prosperity of all': not only a platitude, but an unrealistic statement. 'Economic collaboration with other countries and political appeasement must go hand in hand.' Try that on Hitler and see where it gets you! Harold Nicolson quotes Eden as saying several times throughout 1936 and 1937 that things were really looking up, that the foundations of peace were firmer than many supposed, and that there was no likelihood of war. Eden's main preoccupation and stamping-ground was always Europe. He knew and understood little of the American, Asian and Australasian continents and Black Africa, many of whose affairs were anyway handled by departments other than the Foreign Office. In this he was at one with the inner circle of chic diplomats who kept to an inner circle of posts abroad, consisting basically of Paris, Rome, Madrid and Berlin. Once in a while a posting to Washington, Tehran, Peking or Cairo – where the ambassador was a sort of viceroy – was considered acceptable. Eden, with some knowledge of Middle Eastern languages, did however take a special interest in the Middle East. As I served much of my time in that part of the world I could watch the local effect of his policies. Egypt was a hobby-horse; and Egypt was to prove his undoing.

He considered that a really worthwhile settlement had been achieved in the shape of the Anglo-Egyptian treaty of August 1936. This ended the British military occupation except of the Canal Zone and instituted an alliance for twenty years. Here again the snag was that the treaty did not work out that way. The Egyptians were not madly gratified by the remnants of imperialism which it safeguarded. True, it was reciprocal to the extent that Egyptian warships were promised free access to British ports and facilities and vice versa. It just so happened that there were no Egyptian warships. Eleven years later, when I was in our Cairo embassy, we were only just withdrawing to the Canal Zone. And exactly twenty years later Eden ordered the invasion of Egypt.

By the spring of 1937 Eden's days as Foreign Secretary were numbered. He had no idea that this was so. It was not because of the unbroken series of British diplomatic defeats. His senior colleagues had been in on all these. But he was about to be made the scapegoat. By May Baldwin had had enough of the obloquy. He handed over to the sixty-eight-year-old Neville Chamberlain, who mustered his cronies Simon and Hoare around him on his right and left hands. Once more Eden had misjudged the situation: 'Before Chamberlain became Prime Minister I would think it true that he and I were closer to each other than to any other members of the government.' This simply is not borne out by Chamberlain's own papers.

The hatchet men went to work immediately. Chamberlain decided to run his own foreign policy and selected as the instrument his Chief Industrial Adviser, Sir Horace Wilson, who had absolutely no qualifications for the job. Within a matter of days he and Sir Warren Fisher, the head of the Treasury and the whole Civil Service who, as luck would have it, fell dead a little later in a tart's bedroom, took the extraordinary step of criticising Eden and the FO to Eden's

Parliamentary Private Secretary, J P L Thomas. Obviously they were acting on instructions from their boss. They said that they were thoroughly dissatisfied with the FO and especially with Vansittart. He was an alarmist, he hampered all the government's efforts to make friendly contacts with the dictators, and his influence over Eden was very great. Thomas loyally reported this to Eden, who took it on the chin.

In June 1937 Germany and Italy withdrew from the non-intervention committee. As they had never for a moment acted in accordance with its principles this was a non-event. Far more significant, and sinister, was the first meeting between the attractive and dynamic Italian ambassador, Count Grandi, and Chamberlain. On the strength of it Chamberlain wrote a friendly letter to Mussolini. His own bland comment later was: 'I did not show my letter to the Foreign Secretary, for I had the feeling that he would object to it.'

Eden's comments on the next few months are querulous. 'The two dictators, both ex-servicemen and younger in years, had little respect for elderly non-combatants, as they regarded those who led us.' He is of course referring to his own closest colleagues. When Chamberlain told him that he was not sharp enough with the opposition in parliament he defended himself on the grounds that a Foreign Secretary should remain *au-dessus de la mêlée*. He confesses that he had no idea whether the immediate purchase of anti-aircraft guns in the US or France is possible; 'of course, I admit at once that I am very ignorant of the financial aspect of all this question'. This was in November, within two years of the outbreak of war. At the same time he complained that too high a priority was placed on the mainten-ance of our economic stability, though there were one and a half million unemployed at the time. A small success at the Nyon conference of nine nations convened in September by Britain to deal with piracy in the Mediterranean – the work of 'gentleman' Mussolini – was an encouragement to him.

44

Whoever remembers Nyon today? So he could still pronounce that the principles of the League were the best yet devised for the conduct of international relations because they were entirely in accord with British ideas. This pathetic fallacy was to crop up time and again in the forties and fifties. Alas, the British ideas of Eden and his like had long since lost their effectiveness in the world. As for the League, in November Italy joined the German-Japanese anti-Comintern Pact and in the next month she formally quit the high-minded body which she had flouted for so long.

By now the biggest problem, of Nazi Germany, had to be tackled. Eden was not up to it. When the revolting and stupid Ribbentrop had arrived in August 1936 to be ambassador in London Eden lectured him on his duty to report objectively to his Führer. Not surprisingly, Ribbentrop took the advice in bad part and was 'sulky'. By early 1937 Eden had reached the conclusion on the Sudeten problem that it was not one on which we could properly give more than general advice to the Czechs and the Germans. That is, non-intervention again. In April 1937, a self-inflicted wound: 'I selected Sir Nevile Henderson as the new ambassador to Berlin. The responsibility for this decision was entirely mine.' This is at least candid. Henderson, the pro-Nazi, immediately established a direct line to Chamberlain, bypassing Eden. When Eden resigned in February 1938 Henderson was unable to disguise his delight.

From November 1937 Eden's relations with Chamberlain got speedily worse. Eden made a speech in the Commons which hardly strikes the reader today as unduly firm, but Chamberlain's Parliamentary Private Secretary, Lord Dunglass (alias the Earl of Home and Sir Alec Douglas-Home, an appeaser throughout) reported that the Prime Minister was upset as it would undo much of his conciliatory work especially with Mussolini. Chamberlain now delivered a smack in the eye to Eden. He announced that Lord Halifax would pay an important visit to Berlin. Halifax, earlier as Lord Privy Seal and now as Lord President of the Council, had been told officially to help Eden in the Lords; actually, to keep an eye on him and report to Chamberlain. The absurd pretext was an invitation from Field-Marshal Goering to Halifax, a keen huntsman, to attend some hunting festivities in Germany. Eden was, naturally enough, not keen on the visit but he could not prevent it. Chamberlain expected great things of it. His view was that the FO were unduly hostile to Hitler, and that their methods were too slow for modern times. In this at least he was right. Eden could not refrain from criticising the idea of the visit to Chamberlain and there was an acrimonious exchange. Eventually the Prime Minister of Great Britain told his Foreign Secretary to go home and take an aspirin. Matters had reached such a pitch that Eden's loyal Parliamentary Private Secretary, Jim Thomas, asked Sir Horace Wilson what was really wrong. He got the answer that Chamberlain was unshakable in his policy of getting together with the dictators and genuinely thought he was saving Eden from himself. Halifax went off to Berlin, where the desiccated aristocrat's gross host staged a performance by rutting stags for his pleasure, and at Hitler's behest to Berchtesgaden. He reported on his return that Hitler was very sincere. In other words Halifax was completely hoodwinked. Clearly he was due for promotion, and he soon got it. Eden reflected that his own position had been weakened.

It was at this point that, in order to please Chamberlain, Eden further weakened the hand of the FO. He and Vansittart had been increasingly at loggerheads. As early as 1936 he had tried to shift him to the Paris embassy. Eden visited Cliveden from time to time. In the Cliveden set Ribbentrop's freely expressed view was being echoed: that Van was the only obstacle to understanding with Germany and that 'we are going to have him out'. Van told Eden that he was worried by this association of Eden's – so was Baldwin – and this irritated Eden all the more. He obliged the Cliveden set by kicking Vansittart upstairs to the invented post of Chief Diplomatic Adviser, and the routine was so arranged that

Van could never affect action or decisions but could only ruminate in the void. Van's comment was prophetic: 'I don't like it, Anthony. If I go, you won't last long.' Another member of the Old Etonian club was, naturally, appointed to succeed Van in the shape of Sir Alexander Cadogan. He was a capable official of an absolutely traditional kind. Eden protests that the new arrangement fortified his team. That was certainly not how it struck us junior officials in the Office. We were appalled and bewildered. So were sections of the Press. Chamberlain had won another victory, thanks to Eden's collusion. As a result Eden sincerely felt in January 1938 that the Prime Minister and he were in close agreement about foreign affairs generally. Those whom the gods have decided to ruin they first strike blind.

In reality the internecine struggle was about to reach its climax. One effect of Eden's having to look constantly over his shoulder was that his judgment on matters other than those directly affecting the dictators was impaired. Thus he records vaguely that he often considered our relations with Russia (he prefers that term to 'the USSR') but merely reached the conclusion that she 'can be left for the moment where she is'. If this means anything it expresses an attitude that was not only arrogant but unwise. The only hope, for some years by then, of containing Hitler and Mussolini would have been a sincere and forceful attempt by Britain, France and their allies to get closer to the USSR on the one hand, and the US on the other. They failed in both.

Eden and his diplomats adopted a similarly condescending tone towards the US, which under Roosevelt was striding gigantically forward. Old Sir Ronald Lindsay reported from the fastness of his embassy in Washington that America was 'still extraordinarily youthful and sensitive'. What did he mean by 'extraordinarily'? It seems highly unproductive for this stuffed shirt to comment critically on both youthfulness and sensitivity. And he drew the misleading conclusion that the prestige of Great Britain in 1937 stood so high that 'co-operation with HMG would be regarded as a compliment by the public opinion of even so powerful a state as America' (as he prefers to call the US). He clearly had no idea of the real state of mind of President Roosevelt or the majority of US citizens.

Naturally this showed in our diplomacy. Eden told the US ambassador that he thought the recent Neutrality Act, which forbade the supply of arms to all belligerents, would favour the aggressor and should be changed. This was impertinent on two counts. First, it was the apostle of non-intervention speaking. Secondly, Eden had no right to tell the US government how to run its own affairs. He received the brush-off he deserved. The ambassador replied that the matter was a difficult one of internal politics. Eden did not realise, however, that he had been snubbed. In March 1937 he was capable of writing an extraordinary minute: 'The triangle for us to work in is ourselves, Japan and China, with USA constantly in touch.' So much for France and other loyal friends. And a few weeks later our ambassador to China, Sir Hughe Knatchbull-Hugessen, was punctured by bullets from a Japanese aircraft while about his lawful occasions in China. He survived, received £5000 from parliament for his pains, and went on to be an ambassador in Ankara where the German spy Cicero was able to rifle his safeful of top-secret documents. By then of course Japan had overrun a good deal of the British Empire. Eden never understood the Far East or tried very hard to do so. The FO were no great help over this since the small band of Far East experts were generally regarded as a funny lot of men with more than their fair share of oriental inscrutability.

When Sir Ronald Lindsay was in London in 1936 he discussed with Eden the possibility of his visiting the US. This would have been educational for him, if nothing else. But he never quite found the time. Had our diplomacy made efforts in that direction we might well have received earlier and more whole-hearted support from the US government when war came. But on the contrary we administered a rebuff to President Roosevelt at this very point. He informed HMG in 1937 that he wanted to make a bold pronouncement on peace in the world and asked for Britain's immediate and complete support. The pronouncement was to be in broad and rather vague terms; but from our point of view it was infinitely worth backing the initiative and earning Roosevelt's goodwill.

Eden happened to be away on leave when Roosevelt's message arrived and Chamberlain hastened to deal with it in his own way. Advised by Sir Horace Wilson and Sir Alexander Cadogan he sent a reply which seemed to the US government like a douche of cold water. Eden was outraged when he discovered this on his return. He had a stiff meeting with Chamberlain where it seemed to him that for the first time they were seriously at odds. It cannot have struck Chamberlain in quite that light. He told Eden that the FO were not sincere in their efforts. For the first time Eden noticed that Chamberlain was capable of ruthlessness. He was determined to see the American initiative, and indeed all foreign affairs, only in the context of his projected talks with the dictators. He made it clear that he considered *de jure* recognition of Mussolini's annexation of Abyssinia as having a higher priority. Chamberlain's mouthpiece Wilson dismissed the American proposal as 'woolly rubbish' and in a rage threatened Jim Thomas that if the US government produced the facts he would let loose the full power of the British government machine in an attack on Eden and the FO for the way in which they had frustrated Chamberlain's attempts to save the peace of the world. Eden's reactions were feeble. He conveyed to Wilson that he considered his grasp of foreign affairs less good than of industrial affairs. He sent a wishy-washy further message to President Roosevelt with which, he consoled himself, the President was deeply gratified. But the upshot was that the initiative was never made: 'We had discouraged it to death.' Eden and his colleagues had also much discouraged the President's attempt to be forthcoming and friendly to Britain, and we were to pay for this later. Eden's final comment on this disastrous incident was made in a letter to Lindsay in the style of an industrious civil servant: 'Next time I hope the President will not choose one of my rare leaves to take initiatives with the Prime Minister.' He considered resigning on this important issue but decided against it, partly because Chamberlain insisted that Roosevelt's insistence on secrecy must be respected. Viscount Cranborne, Eden's Under-Secretary, thought that this rebuff to the President would have been the right issue on which to resign, and there is much to be said for his view.

The climax to all this bickering might have appeared farcical if only questions of war and peace had not been at stake. (The same atmosphere was to recur over Suez in 1956.) There was certainly no high tragedy about the way in which it came. Chamberlain wrote a letter to his sister-in-law, Austen Chamberlain's widow, about his conciliatory plans and sent it to her through the ordinary post. This good lady showed the bumptious Foreign Minister, Count Ciano, the letter and he responded: this, he said, was a psychological moment and Mussolini was ready for a settlement. Eden needled Chamberlain by suggesting that Ciano would surely have seen the letter even if Lady Chamberlain had not shown it to him. Chamberlain's response, like that of a US Secretary of State a few years earlier, was that gentlemen do not read each other's mail. But up to the finish Eden was deluding himself. He expressed the view to Grandi that there was now far less danger in Spain of either Bolshevism or Fascism; Grandi readily agreed. Eden was of the opinion that Britain now had a strong moral position – a favourite phrase of politicians when in difficulties – and increasing authority in the world while Mussolini's position was weakening. This was sheer wishful thinking.

After one of the customary long English weekends in February 1938 Eden was annoyed to discover at the FO that Lady Chamberlain had been reading out another of the Prime Minister's letters to Mussolini and Ciano. The Prime

Minister told Eden that Grandi had asked to see him and that he would prefer Eden not to be present. For several days Grandi had deliberately avoided seeing Eden. This time, however Eden insisted on his rights and attended the meeting. Never can a British Foreign Secretary have been in a more humiliating position. Chamberlain played up to Grandi throughout and refused to let his own colleague have his say. Grandi described the two British statesmen as 'two enemies confronting each other, like two cocks in true fighting posture'. When Grandi had gone Chamberlain said that the way was now clear to open conversations with the Italian government at once. Eden demurred. Chamberlain became violent and finally said: 'Anthony, you have missed chance after chance. You simply cannot go on like this.' It was clear that he meant: you simply cannot go on, period.

The *triste farce* continued. Grandi nipped out of Number Ten well satisfied and got into a taxi where a red-faced senior official of the Conservative Central Office, Sir Joseph Ball, was waiting. He had earned his knighthood partly by buying and arranging for the publication of the forged 'Zinoviev letter' at a crucial moment in the 1924 election which helped to ensure a Conservative landslide victory over Labour. He enjoyed dirty work and so did his assistant, Guy Burgess. As Lord Templewood later explained, the Prime Minister for some time 'stepped outside the channel of regular communication' and used this shady figure in his efforts to break the deadlock between the FO and the Italian embassy. He states that the FO were aware of these contacts. Who in the FO, I wonder? Cadogan? Eden himself had not the slightest suspicion.

One more eerie incident took place before Eden actually resigned. Sir John Simon told Jim Thomas that he was as fond of Anthony as if he had been his own son. This alone was enough to send a shudder down the bravest spine. The slimy Simon was notorious for his *fausse bonhomie*; many were the men whose arms he had affectionately taken while addressing them by the wrong Christian name. Jim Thomas, who was later to become Lord Cilcennin, reported to Eden that Simon went on to say that he was sure that Eden was ill.[1] Nothing less than six months' holiday would do, and Thomas must take him away. Thomas answered that Eden had never felt better. Then came the real purpose of Simon's outrageous intervention. It was not the preservation of Eden's sanity. It was that Eden's resignation would be fatal to the government. When Thomas flatly refused to take Eden away Simon gave up. He never addressed a further word to Thomas for over two years.

Chamberlain and Eden had by now decided that he should go, though some members of the Cabinet expressed the view that he had been badly treated. So go he did on 21st February 1938. The customary exchange of letters contained a welter of friendliness and platitudes. Eden's resignation speech was not very effective; above all he felt he could not refer to the disastrous exchanges with Roosevelt. The speech made by Lord Cranborne, today the Marquess of Salisbury, on his simultaneous resignation was much more pointed.[1] 'Why are you going over that, Anthony?' asked Van. 'There is worse to follow, you know. There is Austria.' He was proved right as soon as 12th March. Meanwhile, Chamberlain resumed his talks with Grandi the very day after the resignations.

The truth was that Eden had gone along with the appeasement policy throughout. Part of the time he did so against his will. Whenever he tried an independent line he got rapped over the knuckles by his older and senior colleagues. The occasion of his resignation was not some great question of principle. It was a question of timing and methods limited to only one aspect of our foreign policy. As Vansittart remarked, it was not even the most important aspect. He considered, and rightly, that Italy was a minor front and that the main front remained Berlin. Moreover, Eden did not just resign as a bold gesture. On the contrary, Chamberlain had worked to

[1] *Memoirs,* Earl of Avon.

get rid of him ever since he became Prime Minister. Eden was no match for the old boy in political cunning.

Count Ciano learnt of Eden's fall at a party in Rome and records that there was a general cheer at the news. The Italian Press acclaimed it as a triumph for Mussolini. So it was; he had won that vendetta, as Churchill publicly put it. The general public in Britain, with little knowledge of the inside details or of the past history leading up to the resignation, on the whole applauded his resignation as a brave and justified gesture. Geoffrey Dawson's *Times* was, of course, delighted that he had gone; and Lord Halifax stepped into Eden's shoes without a moment's delay. The staff of the FO and our diplomats abroad were mostly disappointed – Nevile Henderson being an exception – but also mostly ill-informed on the political in-fighting which had taken place. My friends and I were puzzled but on the whole admired Eden's gesture. It was not until I examined the record in detail later on that I realised how misleading the surface picture had been. One third secretary, Con O'Neill, had the courage to resign from his post in Berlin a little later in protest at Henderson's outrageous pro-Nazism. He came back, but turned out later to be a persistent resigner, or contemplator of resignation. The rest of us soldiered on.

One man had been shaken to the core by the affair and his reactions were to mould Eden's subsequent career and indeed life. This was Winston Churchill.

SIX

Profitable Interlude

WINSTON CHURCHILL WAS Eden's dark angel. On the subject of his resignation he wrote with extraordinary emotionalism: 'I had heard something of the serious differences in the Cabinet, though the causes were obscure. I hoped that Anthony Eden would not on any account resign without building up his case beforehand. Late on 20th February 1938 the news reached me. I must confess that my heart sank and for a while the dark waters of despair overwhelmed me. On this night and on this occasion only sleep deserted me. There seemed one strong young figure standing up against the long, dismal, drawling tides of drift and surrender. My conduct of affairs would have been different from his in various ways; but he seemed to me to embody the life-hope of the British nation, the grand old British race. Now he was gone. I watched the daylight slowly creep in through the windows and saw before me in mental gaze the vision of Death.'[1]

The passage is purple indeed; and an example of a great statesman's judgment at its weakest. He reiterated years later to Eden that he never missed a night's sleep throughout the war, but he did on this occasion. He also told him he thought the resignation could have been more effectively handled. In reality the 'strong young figure' (aged forty-one) had, as we have seen, never stood up effectively against the drift. He was far from embodying the life-hope of the grand old British race: he represented only a small section of it which was to become less influential as time went on.

[1] *The Second World War*, 6 vols., Winston S. Churchill, Cassell, 1948–54.

Eden had not even been close to Churchill; nor was he to be until Churchill was firmly in office. Churchill wrote, more moderately, that there had not been much difference in their views and that he 'felt sure his heart was in the right place'. In the resignation debate Churchill fiercely attacked Chamberlain but Eden held back. This was to be the pattern.

It soon became apparent to some of us in the Foreign Office that, even if Eden had achieved disappointingly little, matters would get rapidly worse from now on. Within three weeks of Eden's resignation Hitler took over Austria. Chamberlain's graceless and fatuous comment was that this might well have been avoided if Halifax had become Foreign Secretary earlier. Again Churchill led the opposition to Chamberlain's handling of affairs; again Eden declined to back him. If he had had the courage of his convictions he and Churchill could have led a formidable and effective movement. Instead he formed the 'Eden Group' of Conservatives which reached a total of about thirty. The government's view of their efficacy was expressed in a whip's description of them as 'the Glamour Boys'. Masochistically, Eden would call on Halifax and put forward his ideas. Halifax would listen – he was a polite man, unlike Chamberlain – and do absolutely nothing about them. Eden frequently saw Baldwin at this period and they even dreamed up an alternative government with Eden as Prime Minister. Baldwin warned him against getting involved with Churchill.

Chamberlain now had his way over Abyssinia and in April we recognised Italian sovereignty over that country. In the same month the Sudeten Germans demanded full autonomy, and in July a henchman of Chamberlain's, Lord Runciman, carried out on the spot an examination of the problem with which he was totally unfamiliar and reported in favour of Hitler taking over. Again Churchill thundered; again Eden kept silent. In September Chamberlain, grasping his umbrella, became a sort of commuter to Germany: Berchtesgaden, Godesberg, finally Munich. It was 'peace in our time'. Eden's comment in the House after

Munich, which he does not mention in his own memoirs, was this: 'Perhaps the most encouraging event of all these recent weeks was the warmth of the spontaneous reception in Germany of the Prime Minister. It was clearly a manifestation of the German people's desire for peace. Nobody in this House has ever doubted that desire.' Continuing to curry favour with Chamberlain after the treatment he had received at his hands was undignified to say the least, but that was his own affair. What was terrifying was the entire lack of comprehension on the part of Eden of the Nazi mentality. Hitler duly occupied the Sudetenland in October and Duff Cooper resigned as First Lord of the Admiralty in protest. But, Harold Nicolson records, 'Anthony does not want to defy the Tory Party and is in fact missing every boat with exquisite elegance.'

In December 1938 Eden paid his first visit to the United States. The elegance was evidently to the fore as he was unkindly compared to a film star. The visit made no great impression on Eden, and he seems to have made no great impression on President Roosevelt and his aides. Five years were to pass before he went there again.

Throughout early 1939 the dictators stepped up the pace in the advance to world war. Hitler seized the rest of Czechoslovakia. A country like Bulgaria, where I had been posted in late 1938, was becoming in practice a German protectorate, and our protests were brushed aside. Madrid surrendered to Franco and he had won the civil war. We had already recognised his government. At this time Churchill was pressing for what should have been our policy long before: a military alliance with the USSR. The Soviet government themselves proposed it in April. But the idea was so repugnant to the old gang in the government that they preferred, in concert with France, to give futile and impracticable guarantees of independence to Poland, Romania and Greece. Although Eden was not involved in these guarantees the Polish question became a sort of obsession with him and in the end-of-war inter-Allied

57

arrangements Churchill had to slap him down on the question more than once, since he was holding up much more important matters and annoying both Stalin and Roosevelt at once. However, in May, a glutton for punishment as ever, he volunteered to Halifax to go to Moscow himself. Of course Chamberlain turned him down. At last in August an undistinguished British delegation of military men and diplomats was sent, by slow boat, to discuss possibilities in Moscow. The FO representative was a mere counsellor, William Strang, and the head was called Plunkett-Ernle-Erle-Drax, which is difficult enough in English but impossible to a Russian. Simultaneously Molotov and Ribbentrop were seriously on the job. The 'specific levity' of Britain's attitude to the USSR was by now quite clear to the Soviet government and they chose to sign a non-aggression pact with Germany. They were no doubt wise to do so. They would never have got any sense out of the Chamberlain government. After Germany had invaded Poland on 1st September Chamberlain declared war on Germany on 3rd September in a speech in which the emphasis was as much on his personal disappointment as on the world tragedy.

He clung on to power. With much reluctance he had to call Churchill to the Admiralty, and Eden was tucked away at the Dominions Office without a seat in the Cabinet. He was far from pleased. He was never a great Commonwealth man, though he made the right noises about its members being our loyal allies and so on. He reflected that he had previously been a principal figure in the Cabinet where now he was sometimes called in but never played a full part. But in fact, as we have seen, he had never made the full impact of a Foreign Secretary. And so it was to be again in due course.

There had been hopes in the government, based on nothing at all, that the US would immediately come to our help. In fact she did, but not as wholeheartedly as the optimists anticipated. Why should she, with Chamberlain still at the helm? But Roosevelt amended the Neutrality Act in favour of Britain and France enabling them to purchase arms in the US on a 'cash and carry' basis. The deal under which we received fifty out-of-date destroyers in exchange for long leases of bases in British Caribbean possessions followed on this. We needed those destroyers; but it was a good bargain for Roosevelt all right.

By the end of September 1939 Germany and the USSR had shared out Poland. In the west the small British Expeditionary Force had arrived, with Kim Philby amongst its war correspondents. In December the rump of the League found time to decree the formal expulsion of the USSR. That must have shaken her. And throughout the phoney war our so-called National Government still plodded flat-footedly on. Germany overran Norway and Denmark in April 1940; yet it was not until the very day that she invaded Holland, Luxembourg, Belgium and France – 10th May – that Chamberlain would let go. At last Churchill, at a robust sixty-six, could form a truly national Coalition government including such stalwarts as Attlee, Greenwood, Bevin and Beaverbrook. Out of kindness Chamberlain was kept on as Lord President of the Council until October. Eden was given the War Office, still without a seat in the Cabinet. After Dunkirk in June the King remarked to him one day that he seemed in great spirits and asked why. He replied: 'Now we are all alone, sir. We haven't an ally left.' This was less than fair to the Commonwealth. Nevertheless, I remember that many of us felt this paradoxical relief after our great defeat in the west. But whether it was a sign of statesmanship on the part of our expert in diplomacy is questionable.

'Mai qui fut sans nuages et juin poignardé.' In June the jackal Mussolini declared war on what he reckoned were the failing Britain and France; he and Hitler lived to regret his pointless intervention, and to some extent died of it. Old St John Philby told his mentor King Ibn Saud that Britain could not possibly win and was put inside under article 18B for his pains. Ambassador Kennedy reported similarly to Washington. The US government refused France's desperate

appeal for military aid; Churchill offered France union with Britain, which would indeed have been weird; in the world of hard facts Pétain came to power and signed the armistice with Hitler. In London we came to terms with various exile provisional governments, including the Polish and the Free French under Colonel de Gaulle. In the hostile atmosphere of Bulgaria our small legation staff never seemed to doubt that we should emerge victorious; and the only time I saw our stalwart French colleagues in tears was when they were listening to Churchill's moving asseveration of friendship for France, delivered in his unique version of the French tongue. The US minister showed solidarity by throwing a bottle, accurately, in a nightclub at a German who had objected to the playing of 'Tipperary'.

In that same month of August Eden threatened to resign once more, not too seriously this time. He thought that Churchill was picking on Wavell, our Commander-in-Chief in the Middle East, and told him that he must be more reasonable. Eden went out to Cairo and tried to stop what he considered the folly of diverting men, arms and aircraft to Greece. But – a familiar pattern – Churchill overruled him.

Another familiar characteristic manifested itself in several ways: Eden's proneness to illusions owing to a lack of empathy with other men. Much as he admired Churchill he confessed that he expected that relations might be 'choppy'; however, he comments, this was never the case. In cold fact it was frequently the case, right through to Potsdam and in the years that followed. Again, he was astonished at the Soviet government's cynicism and toughness over the Ribbentrop pact. Why should he have been? They had weighed the matter up carefully, and they certainly owed no gratitude or deference to us. Again, he criticised the US government's hardheadedness over the destroyers-for-bases deal, and on the question of arms being made for us in the US commented that the US administration was pursuing 'an almost entirely American policy, rather than one of all possible aid to Britain'. It is the besetting sin of Eden-style diplomacy, which is still with us today. There is the assumption that everything must be done in the British style, and that the world owes us a living. There is little effort to enter into the psychology and attitudes of other nations because it is considered that they cannot match up with ours. The result is bound to be repeated disappointments and frustration.

In October 1940 Churchill tightened up his administration and finally got rid of Chamberlain. Still no Cabinet post was found for Eden. In November he wished Churchill many happy returns of his birthday with this curiously expressed hope: 'and may we yet celebrate the last stage of a long hard road travelled *la main dans la main.*'

Just before Christmas Eden had his reward. Halifax was sent as ambassador to Washington, where he did surprisingly well for a member of the Chamberlain group. Eden became Foreign Secretary once more. Neither the job nor the relationship with Churchill were to be all that easy. But the close contact was now established, and Eden had reached another turning point in his life where once again Churchill's influence was to be decisive in more ways than one.

SEVEN

The Diplomacy of War

CHURCHILL HAD NO sooner promoted Eden to the War Cabinet than he told him that he must be his successor when the moment came. This was gratifying, but also bewildering, for Eden. Apart from the senior men of his own party who would not have taken kindly to the appointment it seems doubtful whether Attlee, Bevin and others would have agreed to serve under him. And on his record Eden had not shown the calibre of a war leader, or even of a party leader. Nevertheless in 1941 Churchill recommended officially to the King that Eden should succeed if anything happened to him. The painful irony for Eden was that Churchill carried on for fifteen years, playing cat and mouse with him, and only resigned in 1955 when it was, from Eden's point of view, too late.

Moreover Eden found yet again in the great office of Foreign Secretary that he had little independence of action. All the big decisions were taken by Churchill working direct with Roosevelt and Stalin. Eden did not have the weight to put things across with these leaders. Many less important matters were also handled in the same way. Churchill did not hesitate to step in after Eden had in his view mishandled some question and to reverse his policy. This was of course most galling for the Foreign Secretary. In practice he was no more than a sort of Minister of State to Churchill.

For Churchill had taken the FO, and British diplomacy generally, by the scruff of the neck and told them to get a move on. Those carefully thought-out memoranda, presenting lucidly the pros and cons of each measured step, were out. It was a case of one side of a sheet of paper, two or three cogent proposals and conclusions, and action this day. The better type of diplomat responded enthusiastically. The run of the mill footslogged on and were disturbed to find that the tempo was being accelerated by recruits of all ages from the real world outside Whitehall, where business was business. Certainly Eden, Cadogan and their ilk worked hard and conscientiously. But they were hardly the hustlers whom Churchill demanded to have at his beck and call. Eden would serve up a beautifully drafted memo presenting the pros – 'on the one hand' – and the cons – 'on the other hand'. The Marquess of Salisbury had commented mildly on the FO drafting style a full generation earlier: 'Ah, how well I know those hands!' Churchill's comment, already quoted, was more lavatorial.

In early 1941 there were few signs of the improvement in the anti-axis coalition which was to manifest itself by the end of the war, chiefly owing to the crass policy of the axis itself in forcing that coalition to get cracking. Eden went again to Cairo and when he returned to London the Balkans and the Middle East were in chaos. The Germans advanced peacefully into Bulgaria and parked their tanks opposite our legation in Sofia. Our Minister protested, on instructions from the Foreign Office, to the wily King Boris who still maintained that Bulgaria was fully independent. This foxy king later got his deserts from his patron, Hitler, who arranged for his demise. He was not as clever as he thought at playing off great powers against each other. When we broke off relations and left in a special diplomatic train for Turkey the Germans kindly gave us a parting present of two large time bombs, one of which blew a great hole in the Istanbul hotel where we were staying and killed several people. When Yugoslavia tried to turn against them she was mercilessly overrun. Rommel arrived in the desert and advanced swiftly. We had to evacuate Greece. For a time Iraq and Syria were in enemy hands. I was well placed to observe all these happenings from my new post in our Embassy in Ankara. Turkey remained staunchly 'neutral' on our side, and became a great stamping ground for spies of all nations. Eden remarks, in familiar style, at this stage, that Middle Eastern problems were submitted to 'a useful discussion' in the FO with a 'general consensus' being reached in the end though the plan for action was rather a gamble; as if the whole war were not a gigantic gamble.

In the US two decisive steps were taken at this time. Against strong opposition President Roosevelt pushed through his Lend-Lease Act in March 1941. This made all the difference to the supply of American arms to the Western allies and later to the Soviet Union. And in secret the great Manhattan Project began the operations which were to produce the nuclear weapon before Hitler – or Stalin – could do so. However, Eden's attitude to the Americans was no more forthcoming than usual. When expressing keen admiration for the qualities of de Gaulle – though they were never close collaborators – he cannot resist taking a poke at the Americans: if we, he reflects, had been as tenacious and even contumacious as de Gaulle was, some of the Anglo-American troubles of later years might have been avoided. In May he told US ambassador Winant, a staunch friend of Britain, that in his view American opinion was flagging for want of a lead. This presumptuous statement was duly reported to the President who indicated to Ambassador Halifax that he did not care for it. Eden was also indignant about rumours in the US that we were negotiating secretly with Hess who had flown into Scotland. When Harry Hopkins said clearly that Roosevelt intended to come into the war on our side Eden's reaction was to shudder at the possibility of another 'Wilsonian' interference in an eventual European settlement. Meanwhile, however, the Former Naval Person who was now our Prime Minister had established cordial direct relations, which might even justify that overworked description 'a special relationship', with the President. They met for the first time in the middle of the Atlantic in August and collaborated to produce the ringing declaration of the Atlantic Charter. Considering the stiff opposition to involvement inside the US this was a courageous and forthcoming step by Roosevelt.

Throughout May and June we received increasing intelligence of a huge German build-up against their Soviet ally. As the date approached Churchill ordered that Ambassador Maisky in London should be given the information on which we based our expectation of a German attack. When Eden spoke to Maisky on 13th June he did not succeed in shaking Maisky's apparent scepticism, though Maisky was better informed on the number of German divisions deployed on the eastern front. When Germany did attack on 22nd June, and thus made us a present of a formidable ally without whom we might not have survived as a free nation, Eden seems to have expected that the Russians would come running to embrace us. That was a time for hardheadedness rather than gestures though Churchill's broadcast promise, made on the very day of the attack, of all aid to the USSR made a favourable impression in that country. At that moment Sir Stafford Cripps forecast that the USSR might hold out for up to four weeks, while the Chief of the Imperial General Staff, Field-Marshal Sir John Dill, gave her seven. Eden did not hazard a guess.

Eden's obsession with Poland caused him to push the question of Soviet relations with the exiled government in London into the forefront even when the USSR was fighting for its life. General Sikorski, the head of that powerless administration, was encouraged to put forward his conditions for co-operation. The discussions all took place in cloudcuckooland. Eden was satisfied because in July a piece of paper called an agreement was signed. It settled nothing and the Russians were glad to get the question temporarily out of the way in this manner.

But while Eden was always embarrassed at having the Russians as allies the British people were delighted. In September a 'Russian Tank Week' was enthusiastically worked in our arms factories. There were calls for a second front – quite impossible at the time – to ease the pressure on the Soviet Union. The dynamic Lord Beaverbrook and Averell Harriman had stiff but productive talks in Moscow arranging for war supplies from the West. Since Iran was required as one supply route and the old Shah showed no signs of co-operating, an agreed invasion by Soviet forces from the north and British from the south took over the country and expelled the Shah. Though Eden saw the need for this he accepted it reluctantly.

December was to produce another decisive turning point. On the 7th the Japanese ensured US participation in the war by smashing up Pearl Harbor. Churchill decided that we should immediately join the US in declaring war on Japan. This decision put at risk, and in fact led to the loss of, a large part of our empire; but it clinched the massive support for us world-wide of the US, without which we could not have won. I am sure that Churchill was right. The US responded by declaring war on Germany and Italy. Churchill felt it was time for him to visit Roosevelt again. Meanwhile Eden had left for Moscow with the purpose, as he put it, of assuring Stalin that we and the US would not ignore Russian interests in the post-war settlement. Matters were not to turn out in that way. Eden acquired the habit of referring either to 'Mr Stalin' or 'the Bear'. The latter was a quote from the Victorian song which gave rise to the term 'jingoism', meaning extreme imperialism:

> *We don't want to fight but by jingo if we do*
> *We've got the men, we've got the arms . . .*

The state of mind which this reveals in Eden could not possibly appeal to either Stalin or Roosevelt. When robustly used by Churchill it seemed less offensive. Eden was to refer to 'the Bear' for the last time during the Suez imbroglio, with disastrous results.

Eden represented to Churchill that they should not both be out of the country at the same time, but he was overruled. Churchill had faith in Attlee and the rest. Churchill put the case with his usual bluntness and perspicacity: the emphasis of the war had now shifted and what mattered was the intentions of our two great allies. Eden was not so clear. In Moscow he again allowed the Polish question to bedevil his talks with Stalin and Molotov. However Stalin agreed to a friendly communiqué at the end. Eden also accepted, with reluctance, the fact that the US must 'in time' become the dominant partner in our relationship but considered flatly that this was not yet the case. It was the old trouble of Eden's and our diplomacy preferring not to look facts in the face. He criticised not only the Americans, for instance when their Chiefs of Staff's strategy differed, naturally enough, from ours, but also Churchill for going along too often with them. He specifically criticised Roosevelt for his increasing tolerance of Soviet political demands – Poland again – as their victories became vaster. Soviet policy he found amoral, while US policy was exaggeratedly moral at least where non-American interests were concerned. Here we go again. British standards are the best and should be copied by all. The first part of the syllogism is doubtful, the second simply unreal. If Eden had had his way they'd all have been out of step bar our Charlie. This eventually happened over Suez.

During 1942 the war went a great deal worse before it got better. The Japanese were rampaging all over south-east Asia. The Germans pressed on in the Soviet Union. Tempers became frayed in Britain. Churchill, while still recommending Eden as his successor, ambiguously gave Attlee the official title of Deputy Prime Minister and Attlee took a constant hand in foreign policy. When Eden went off to a conference in Cairo he was surprised that Churchill joined him two days later; but not all the members of the Cabinet were so surprised. Eden was now Leader of the House and was reproached by Churchill on one occasion for his 'febrile' behaviour. He confessed he felt too tired to consider post-war problems and handicapped by his lack of economic knowledge. The vendetta with John Foster Dulles began in a small way. Dulles was in London on a semi-official exploratory mission. Eden's comment was that, while he was interested to have the US's views on the future, our own were more important as regards Europe. The US knew very little about Europe; they were uninstructed on the subject. This was yet another vendetta that Eden was to lose.

In July it came to a bitter vote of censure debate in the Commons about the direction of the war. In August came Churchill's 'surprise' visit to join Eden in Cairo, from where Churchill went on to Moscow and conferred with Stalin and Harriman, now US ambassador there. In the same month Churchill's Cairo visit had the decisive effect of placing Generals Alexander and Montgomery in charge in the Middle East. In October came El Alamein, and a crucial corner was turned – for the government, for Britain, and for the world. Eden, who always fancied that he was particularly adept at relations with the French, expressed his indignation at the Americans' recognition of Admiral Darlan as French head of state in North Africa after the Germans had occupied the rest of France. Yet there was much to be said in favour of this as a tactical move. In any case Darlan was assassinated on Christmas Eve and it was left to Churchill, Roosevelt and their aides, including Eden, to bring about a shot-gun wedding between de Gaulle and General Giraud at Casablanca in January 1943. In the long run it is difficult to say who offended the touchy de Gaulle more: Roosevelt with his hardly concealed aversion for a man who was both powerless and proud, or Eden who was to insult and hector his French allies in 1956 over Suez. We are all reaping the whirlwind to this day. In January 1943 occurred also the most portentous setback to the axis in Europe. The Russian counter-offensive at Stalingrad, begun two months before, crushed the axis forces and Field-Marshal von Paulus surrendered.

During 1942 Eden had decided, perhaps partly from frustration on larger matters, to take in hand the reform of the FO, Diplomatic and Consular Services. He was ill-fitted for the task. Sir Stafford Cripps proposed that the framework should be an amalgamation of the FO, Dominions and Colonial Offices. This was clearly a sensible idea which would have abolished the trichotomy in our overseas relations which, surviving from our imperialist days, was a constant handicap and also a source of puzzlement to our allies such as the Americans. But Eden was not prepared to go so fast. Bevin tried again later and also failed; and even today the Commonwealth Office have only just given up their jealous and debilitating independence. However, Eden's modest reforms, presented as almost a revolution though none of us saw it in that light, changed the name of our FO overseas services to the Foreign Service – not in honour of the US Foreign Service but because no handier name came to mind – and stipulated that diplomats, consuls and commercial officials should be interchangeable.

Also, although officials would continue to be known as counsellors, second secretaries and so on when abroad, they would officially be 'Grade A 6' or 'Grade B 4' officers and so on. It was all a distinction without a difference. Recruiting from the usual sources was not affected one way or the other, and certainly not improved. Where diplomats and consuls had failed to mix on equal terms before, they continued to fail to do so now. A few consuls occupied diplomatic posts and in return a very occasional diplomat became a commercial or an information official. 'Grade B officers' continued to have chips on their shoulders. These reforms, in the sacred name of democratisation, became law in 1943 and Bevin duly put them through when the war had ended. Within twenty years we were back with HM Diplomatic Service, and although a few further and inadequate reforms had been effected Eden's efforts were sunk almost without trace and the Service was still not equipped to deal with the world in the sixties, let alone seventies.

At Casablanca the crucial decision had been taken that all our enemies must surrender unconditionally. This was much criticised later on the grounds that it drove them to prolonged resistance whereas the war could have been shortened by a negotiated peace. I have never agreed with that view. Nazi Germany had to be smashed and her government handed over entirely to the allies. In some ways the enduring results are not too good, but they would have been worse if she had been left in one piece. In any case the USSR would not have allowed this, and she fully agreed with the principle of unconditional surrender. Today we see two prosperous Germanys and a very prosperous Japan indeed. And to the anti-axis allies at the time it was an inspiring watchword and a clear definition of what we must achieve.

After Casablanca Churchill went on to Cairo and Turkey. This was a great excitement for us in the embassy there. He conferred with the Turkish president, Inönü, in a train at a small place called Adana in the middle of Anatolia or, in other words, of nowhere. Churchill pressed Inönü and his melodiously named ministers Sararcoglu and Menemencoglu to plunge into the war on our side. All top Turkish statesmen at that time suffered from deafness. These three had this diplomatic faculty particularly well developed, and it gave them extra time to reflect while propositions and questions were repeated to them. In fact they reflected until allied victory was quite certain, and I think they were right from our point of view as well as theirs. They might have been overrun by the Germans from Bulgaria – their army was largely horse-drawn and their air defences were negligible – whereas they remained as increasingly friendly and valuable 'neutrals' on our side. Amongst other facilities we exploited an admirable spying base here (one of our agents, who must be nameless, was perhaps the most distinguished man in the whole history of espionage). So, of course, did the enemy. Not for many months did we catch up with Ambassador von Papen's man Cicero, who in the intervals of butlering in the embassy dining-room was nipping into the ambassador's study next door and taking admirable photographs of top-secret documents from the safe which was often left negligently open. As Ankara (which we still called Angora, like the rabbit) was considered one of the key embassies during the war we were kept exceptionally fully informed by the Foreign Office and neighbouring missions of important diplomatic and military developments and plans everywhere. Thus it was that Cicero was able to procure, and despatch, via von Papen to Berlin, facsimiles of all our plans for Overlord, the invasion of Europe. I learnt later from a German lady who was a secretary in Hitler's chancellery at the time that the rival intelligence organisations in Berlin quarrelled so much over the authenticity of these priceless documents that it was finally decided to ignore them. But this was some little way ahead. As for our careless ambassador Sir Hughe Knatchbull-Hugessen, otherwise 'Snatch,' he carried on regardless and was rewarded with a further comfortable embassy. Security was not taken very seriously in our missions in those days. When Churchill returned to Britain from Turkey he had a brush with Eden over the visit. He told him he had resented his enlisting the War Cabinet into advising against it. He must be able to go where he wanted. President Roosevelt had been astonished that he should be hampered in this way. The FO were always on about fiddling details like the preemption of Turkish chrome. 'There is old Anthony thinking all I want is a joy ride. He has got it all wrong.'

Eden also got one or two things wrong in connexion with the post-war settlement and the part that the US intended to play. In the House he laid down two conditions for any international organisation. First, it should represent the powers that meant to keep the peace. This was harking back to the League of Nations. The United Nations charter does indeed include many references to peace. But the difficulty is that there always have been and will be powers which prefer not to keep the peace. You have to choose between a universal and permissive organisation, which the UN has become, and which can have considerable value in its own way; or one completely dominated by a few strong powers with effective means of punishing miscreants. In fact this was what Eden had in mind, for his second condition was that the organisation must have force to give effect to decisions. In post-war circumstances this combination was rendered quite impossible by the fact that the super and great powers were at loggerheads amongst themselves. The nearest Eden's ideas came to realisation was in organisations such as NATO and the Warsaw Pact, a very different kettle of fish from his beloved League but at least more practical in keeping the peace.

President Roosevelt wanted to take a good look at Churchill's aide and summoned him over on his own in March 1943. Eden found much to puzzle and disturb him in American policy. For a start he seemed surprised that the President intended to 'keep the US in the forefront' after the war. Eden found that his proposals were often at odds with the President's. Roosevelt never concealed his dislike of imperialism and colonialism, both British and French; while we, and even the shattered French, still deluded ourselves that we should maintain our empires after the war. Even Churchill, who got along well with Roosevelt, was shocked at his suggestion later on that we should hand Hong Kong back to China. With all we had on our plate we became further involved in what Eden calls 'a running fight' with the US government over France's territories. Roosevelt could not stand de Gaulle at any price, and right up to and including Potsdam we took it on ourselves to speak up for him. Eden was further surprised that the President took the Polish question calmly. The three great powers would have to agree on a solution and Poland would have to accept, he said. He would also agree to the USSR's demands on the Baltic States and Finland. On Germany he favoured dismemberment; Eden was inclined to agree. Eden lectured the President and Hopkins about our import programme which he said they must regard 'as a first charge that had to be fulfilled'. This was no way to talk to our most powerful ally.

It must have offended all the more because of a small but significant incident that had occurred shortly before. Sir Kingsley Wood, Chancellor of the Exchequer, had written to his opposite number Henry Morgenthau, the Secretary of the Treasury. Mrs Eleanor Roosevelt came down on Wood like a ton of bricks. She said that the letter was addressed 'with that touch of arrogance the British sometimes have' in that it omitted the official title of the recipient. She would not accept a plea of 'ignorance not arrogance' or an explanation that we do things differently. 'The British know quite well that at times they think our American customs do not conform with the ordinary amenities and we know quite well that they think our customs and habits are different. Each country should try to know what the other thought right, and it does no harm for us to know both our weaknesses and our differences', she wisely commented. But such important subtleties were way above the heads of most British diplomats, including Eden. One exception was Macmillan who was doing excellent work as Minister of State in liaison with the US High Command in North Africa. This was to stand him in good stead in 1956 and subsequently. Macmillan's chief complaint was that he could get no policy guidance from the FO, but he managed very well all the same.

Eden also had some talks in Washington about progress on the atom bomb, evidently without realising how much it would change the character of diplomacy. Altogether Eden found the conversations 'perplexing'. Yet Roosevelt and his colleagues spoke frankly and gave fair warning of the issues on which they and we would differ. If he did not say in terms that he thought US-Soviet relations the most important of all he went pretty far to suggest it. This was a conception which Eden found it very difficult to hoist in. He thought he detected a dichotomy between the modern-minded President and Under-Secretary Sumner Welles on the one hand, and the traditionalist Secretary of State Cordell Hull on the other. There was a certain dichotomy over British diplomacy too; but oddly enough the more realistic and modern-minded character in this case was the older one, Churchill.

No sooner was Eden back in London than Churchill took two steps. He pressed him hard to become Viceroy of India; but Eden declined to be sidetracked and Field-Marshal Earl Wavell, of whom Churchill never thought highly, was appointed instead. Then Churchill went off on his own for a long visit to Washington, where he no doubt checked on the impression made by Eden. Under Roosevelt's influence Churchill telegraphed to his colleagues asking whether de Gaulle should not be eliminated as a political force. The Cabinet were all against it and Attlee and Eden replied accordingly. Eden was much incensed by the President's attitude which he described as 'hysterical'. He even compared his obstinacy to that of Hitler at Stalingrad. He was shocked at the idea that France should not be restored as a great imperial power and deluded himself that she would have more of a say in European affairs than the US. He was all against subservience to the US and considered Churchill guilty of this. When he had finished his prolonged business in Washington Churchill flew to North Africa with General George Marshall, and summoned Eden there for the fag-end of his journey. In August 1943 however Eden was included in the party at Quebec where the main topic was Far Eastern strategy. A by-product was that in spite of all the fuss that had gone before – and was to follow – the US government joined us in recognising the French Committee for National Liberation in Algiers, which included Generals Giraud and de Gaulle. In July Mussolini had fallen, and in early September General Eisenhower announced Italy's unconditional surrender.

In October Eden was sent to Moscow to one of those conferences of allied Foreign Ministers that always seemed a little unreal as it was evident that the decisions could only be taken by their masters. Six months before the Soviet government had broken off relations with the Polish govern-

75

ment in exile in London, which by now was a bit of a phantom anyway. Nevertheless Eden flogged on about Poland as he saw it. Molotov was polite but non-committal; 'old Hull', as Eden discourteously calls him, was much the same. Eden achieved nothing, though he heads a long chapter in his memoirs: 'Concern for Poland'. He thought Stalin looked 'more and more like bruin.' However Stalin appreciated the force of our contribution to the war effort. Eden felt that the Americans were claiming too much credit for their share in the great combined bomber offensive and that one object was to 'dim our glory'. It is an odd way of writing history. The RAF certainly earned glory unlimited. So did the United States Air Force, and as time went on their contribution became more massive than any. One result of the Foreign Ministers' meeting was the setting up of the European Advisory Commission to plan the post-war organisation of Europe. This was a good propaganda effort against Germany and her friends eighteen months before their defeat. Eden and the FO took it to be, more than that, a body which could and would neatly sort out all Europe's problems in the west, centre and east. Of course it never achieved anything of the kind.

Eden was hardly back from the preparatory Moscow meeting when he was off again with Churchill to meet President Roosevelt and President Chiang Kai-shek in Cairo. He found this gathering frustrating and boring. At one point Churchill accused him of being sulky and bad-tempered. For his part he was amazed at the patience with which Churchill handled Roosevelt. Then on to Tehran, where for the first time Stalin was lured out of his lair. This was the first of the seminal big-three conferences that shaped the post-war world. Eden's comment? From his own point of view Poland and Turkey were the most important subjects. Roosevelt, of course, was not helpful on Poland. He told Stalin that for electoral reasons he could not discuss it for another year, or in other words intimated that Stalin should go ahead with whatever his plans were. Eden still worked for a settlement which the Poles could accept; that is, his private set of Poles in London, whom Stalin did not recognise anyway. He could not fathom why the Americans did not gang up with us against Stalin. The truth of the matter, which Churchill understood perfectly, was that Roosevelt was making an all-out effort to get a sound basis for general collaboration with Stalin. This sometimes implied leaving the weakest of the three, Britain, a little bit out of it. He was surely right to make the effort. Churchill resented it at times but was big enough to appreciate the overall plan. He was certainly not prepared to hamper it for the sake of a Poland which did not exist and whose future seemed increasingly certain to depend on the Soviet Union.

Briefly back in Cairo in December 1943 Eden got on the wrong side of both Churchill and Roosevelt on two issues of moderate importance. He upset the President so much over his handling of the exiled King of Greece that Roosevelt complained bitterly to Churchill. On Yugoslavia, where Churchill had grasped the importance of Tito, Eden was still working for a compromise including the return of the monarchy, to which the partisans were unalterably opposed. Eden deluded himself that the Russians would help to find such a compromise.

In January 1944 the Soviet government replied to a proposal for negotiations with the London Poles in a manner that seemed to Eden like a blow in the face. The reason soon became clear: a couple of months later the Red Army stormed across the frontier into Poland. Eden began to despair: 'It is no doubt good that many papers should be prepared but this seems an occasion for action and I should like a meeting to discuss it.' He felt strongly that we could not go on waiting for the US. Churchill however continued reluctant to be at odds with the President whenever it could be avoided. He also continued to champion Tito, who, remarks Eden, in September levanted from British protection at Viš and flew to Moscow. 'The Communist had homed to his lair, which nearly became his cage.' Not only is the comment malicious towards Churchill. It shows a complete misunderstanding of Tito's character and effectiveness.

By now the thousand-year Reich was cracking on all fronts. The Normandy landings took place successfully on 6th June. In July the Soviet government recognised their own tame Poles, the so-called Lublin Committee of Polish Liberation who operated in Moscow, as the authority for liberated Poland. In August we opened yet another front on the French Riviera, while de Gaulle entered Paris in the wake of his allies' troops and set up his Provisional Government there. In September the Americans crossed the frontier into Germany.

It was clearly time for another round of talks between the anti-axis allies about post-war arrangements. Churchill went to Quebec in September to meet Roosevelt, and Eden joined the party for its closing stages. He had an open altercation with Churchill in the President's presence. Roosevelt had, without giving the matter much thought, approved the Morgenthau plan which called for the complete de-industrialisation of Germany and her segmentation into numerous small units. Churchill agreed. Eden, who had earlier favoured a plan on these lines, said he did not. This was the only occasion Eden could recall on which Churchill showed impatience with him before foreign representatives. (His memory was at fault on this point.) But a number of top Americans, including Hull, did not like the plan either. They and Eden had their way and the plan was shelved. It is tempting to speculate what its effects would have been. I feel sure that the Russians would in any case have set up their own sort of state in the east.

In October Eden accompanied Churchill to Moscow and had the 'creepy' experience of meeting the Lublin Poles. The more victoriously the might of the two super-powers was deployed, and the nearer the new era came, the more difficult it became for Eden and the FO regulars to grasp developments. He descends to vituperation. The Lublin Poles look like 'rats and weasels'. Roosevelt, having been reelected President for the fourth time in November, sends 'three bad messages'. He is 'snarky' and arrogant.[1] Stalin was now the only one of the Big Three who has a clear view of what he wants; Churchill is all emotion, Roosevelt vague and jealous of others. It was in this mood that Eden approached the decisive meetings of Yalta in February and Potsdam in July 1945. He was almost at the end of his tether. One Cabinet meeting was 'intolerable', and he was in a bloody temper because his colleagues would draft his own messages for him. He was so tired that for almost a week he made very little sense in the House. When he suggested to Churchill, in good bureaucratic fashion, that the Foreign Secretaries and their staffs should meet before the Big Three and draw up an orderly agenda, Churchill slapped him down. In a preliminary talk with the new US Secretary of State, Stettinius, he finds as usual that the Americans give too little weight to Poland.

Eden was out of his depth at Yalta, which in effect laid down the spheres of influence of the Soviet Union on the one hand and the Western allies on the other, though the phrase has always been officially taboo. Again most of his time was devoted to Poland. One evening he and his FO men produced a good draft which the Russians refused to consider. 'So I fairly let them have it.' That of course had not the slightest effect. How could it? Little bits of papers could hardly weigh in the balance against the might of the Red Army which had liberated Poland from the Nazis. At a 'terrible' dinner the President was vague and loose, and Churchill made no less than two long speeches. In a discussion on the Far East Eden has an open disagreement with Churchill, who as usual had his way. He admits that he should not be fretted so much by little things, and that he flounders when discussing economic matters. After Yalta the Soviet government's attitude appears to harden on all matters; he can only wonder why. There were at least two important categories of reason. One was that the Soviet forces were

[1] *Memoirs,* Earl of Avon.

winning victory after victory. Another was that, thanks to their network of spies, including Donald Maclean at our embassy in Washington and Philby in London, they were receiving invaluable intelligence on American nuclear developments, which they both feared and were determined to match on their own.

There had been one interlude which Eden had enjoyed. Over Christmas 1944 he had visited Athens with Churchill to see how our forces there were handling the Communist attempt at a takeover. Even here Eden had grumbled at not being allowed to go on his own, and at Churchill negotiating with Archbishop Damaskinos when it was really his job. Even the impassive Cadogan who accompanied them remarked that he had never bargained to take both Tettrazini and Melba all over the place in one party. Of the three countries we had 'guaranteed' so unwisely in 1939 Poland and Rumania had disappeared into the Soviet sphere; Greece was on the brink and Churchill and Eden were determined to save her, in spite of widespread criticism that we were interfering in her internal affairs. So we were, but in a good cause and a practicable one. Eden comments arrogantly about the Greek leaders, particularly of course the Communists but the others as well. But he becomes sentimental, even incoherent, about our soldiers. 'Nothing gives me more comfort than when a soldier's face lights up with pleasure when he recognises one. The truth is that I like our people and to be with them. . . . I prefer the quiet welcome of our English boys. They are splendid. It would be the highest honour to serve and lead such men. . . . Anything to do with men is always intriguing and I always seem to have to do with papers.'[1] He was in a dilemma. His gift had never been and never would be for dealing with men, whether his British colleagues, his foreign colleagues, his class equals or his class inferiors. He was good with paper. But *la paperasserie* is not the same as effective diplomacy, particularly when you are dealing with young and vigorous peoples, and

[1] *Memoirs,* Earl of Avon.

particularly in the mid-twentieth century. Perhaps after all he should have devoted himself to military matters. He had been a courageous officer and a good War Secretary for a brief time in 1940, and he often felt nostalgia for the military style.

On 12th April President Roosevelt, who had looked like death at Yalta and had been far from functioning at full throttle, was stricken down. He was succeeded by Harry S Truman who was regarded by many people as a joke and who rapidly developed into a strong and admirable President. A week later the Russians battered their way into Berlin, by kind permission of the Western allies who could have taken it earlier but held back. The same occurred over Prague and Budapest. Hitler died in Berlin on 30th April and Berlin surrendered on 2nd May. The Russians had already flown in from Moscow a small, tough man with a goatee beard called Ulbricht. He set about organising East Germany and he has been at it ever since, with marked efficiency in his way.

Even if Eden's nerves were frayed by now he had stood up well physically to the rigours of his wartime responsibilities. At the end of May however his doctor diagnosed a duodenal ulcer and he had to take several weeks' complete rest on the eve of the General Election campaign. The Labour members of the government were anxious to get an electoral decision; so was Churchill, who was confident of victory. Within three weeks of VE Day on 8th May Churchill formed a Conservative caretaker government to carry on until the election planned for 26th July. Eden suffered a most bitter blow in May when his elder son was killed with the RAF in Burma.

His musings on the internal political scene at this point show a similar vagueness to that of his approach to the new diplomacy. How, he wondered, could he lead the ordinary men of Britain through party politics? Most of them, he thought, had no party feelings; just as he believed he had none. He was to have a shock on this point. However, he was ready to be labelled a left-wing Tory. There was a move by some Tories to get Churchill out before the election; Eden could not support this. He doubted whether he could continue at the FO, not so much because of the work itself but because of 'the racket with Winston at all hours'. Well, the question was not going to arise, for six years at any rate.

Eden's comments on Potsdam, which lasted from 17th July to 2nd August, are in tune with the old refrain. We must show independence towards the Americans, who did not understand Europe. He deplores Churchill's agreement with Truman to recognise the new Polish government. Churchill was under Stalin's spell again. The possibility of the Tories losing the election crossed his mind: 'if it were not for the immediate European situation I am sure it would be better thus' – an arrogant assumption that only he and his Tory colleagues could cope with European problems, or indeed diplomacy as a whole. Then in the middle of the conference the Labour landslide was announced: Labour 412 seats, the Conservatives 213, the Liberals 12. So those splendid chaps in the forces had some political feelings after all. They wanted the old gang out. After all, there had been no General Election since 1935 – ten very long and formative years. Churchill offered Attlee the services of the indispensable diplomat Eden. They were not required.

However, more important events than these had occurred at Potsdam. The rigid division of Europe, and Germany, into Western and Communist spheres of influence was confirmed. The only enclave was the western part of Berlin; and here the Americans and British out of the kindness of their hearts gave up a sector to the French, just as they gave a zone in West Germany. But above all President Truman, having told Churchill on 17th July of the successful explosion of the first atomic bomb a fews day earlier, conveyed the same message to Stalin on 24th July. This was received with a nod of the head, a brief 'thank you', and no comment. Stalin was probably aware of the explosion already from his secret sources and was waiting to see how long it would be before his ally vouchsafed the information. But in a sense

Truman might almost as well have dropped the bomb on the conference table. The man of steel had led his people through indescribable hardships and at a loss of twenty million Russians to victory. Now the Americans, whom he in no way trusted in spite of all Roosevelt's efforts, had the weapon which could, if things went wrong, endanger all the bitterly won Soviet gains and the homeland itself. Stalin, who was the only one of the Big Three to go through both Yalta and Potsdam from beginning to end, had decided at Yalta on a hard line everywhere in the world and in every context, giving not an inch and pressing forward wherever this could be done with advantage while his scientists and spies sweated their guts out to bring about the construction of the Soviet nuclear weapon. At Potsdam he served notice that the Cold War was on with a vengeance, and that it would in some ways be more perilous than the World War which was just ending.

For Churchill and Eden the days, weeks and months following on the election were almost unbearably bitter. They had after all played a large part in leading Britain from defeat to victory only to see themselves summarily dismissed by the people. As happens on several occasions in the Eden story tragedy mingled with farce. How ridiculous that he and Churchill should have to give up representing Britain in the middle of one of the world's most important conferences! Bad timing of the election was to blame there. But Eden must have asked himself more broadly: what had gone wrong? Britain had fought longer than anyone against Hitler and with great courage and effect. Now, instead of being number one power in the world she looked like being number three. Of course she was small compared with the US and the USSR, but she had her great empire.

The truth is that British diplomacy in the 1930s was much to blame. It was not only the appeasement policy but what lay behind it. Relying on traditions and an empire which, in both cases, were breaking up, our diplomats reckoned to carry on coping with Europe by paying lip service to the somewhat fly-blown Entente Cordiale while paying no attention at all either to our own relative economic situation nor, either economically or politically, to the great new potential of the US and the USSR. And so we were chased clean out of Europe and had to struggle painfully back with the help of these two powers.

In reflecting on the wartime years Eden writes: 'My experience of likes and dislikes of personalities is that they may make the work of diplomacy congenial or tedious but they do not influence policy. After years of practice it is almost instinctive to treat the work to be done as an exercise.' On the substance our diplomacy got it all wrong in the 1930s. Together with that it got the methods wrong too. It was precisely the personality of Churchill, and his understanding and handling of other personalities, that achieved such diplomatic successes as we had in the war. In one way the diplomacy of war is less complicated than everyday diplomacy. Your basic resources and potential are pretty clearly defined; so are those of your allies and your enemies. Moreover you must have victories. In everyday diplomacy victories are dangerous; they can lead to resentment that is perhaps swallowed but regurgitated at an awkward moment later on. However, even everyday diplomacy in the conventional manner is bound to be sadly at a loss in the world since the Second World War. Diplomacy in this period has had to deal with a world constantly at war; but a new and complicated sort of war. As the last official shots were fired was our diplomacy going to show that we had learnt nothing and forgotten nothing? Would we return with a sigh of relief to the neat minutes, memoranda and negotiations which once had formed an apparently adequate substitute for action and for effective relationships? The alternative would call for constant initiative and energy. And many of Britain's leaders, officials, and just people were, like Eden, exhausted and in varying degrees frustrated.

EIGHT

In Opposition

CHURCHILL WAS NOW seventy. His amazingly robust constitution had brought him through the war in good fettle but
the couple of heart attacks he had suffered, apart from other
ailments, did not make him fighting fit for a long haul in
opposition. He might well have stepped down gracefully,
and profitably for his party, in favour of his acknowledged
number two, Eden, who was forty-eight. A mixture of reasons
held him back. On the positive side, he had run the whole
show so completely from 1940 to 1945, and still felt so capable
of carrying on, that he felt it his duty – and pleasure – to do
so. On the negative side, he himself had not become Prime
Minister until he was in his sixties and thought young Eden
could well wait; and by now he had his doubts about Eden's
personality and, as time went on, health.

Neither Churchill nor, particularly, Eden was well suited
to opposition. They began in a bitter and surprised mood.
Although the Labour leaders had collaborated wisely and
fruitfully throughout the war it had never occurred to the
Tory leaders that anyone but they could or should be called
upon when victory was won to resume the advance towards
Britain's past glory. Churchill pronounced that he would not
preside at the dissolution of the British Empire. Eden began to
build up in his memory the image of his own, and Britain's,
gallant stand against the dictators in the 1930s. In both cases
these were sad delusions. The empire was, by historical
necessity, on the way out. Britain, and Eden, had never
stood up successfully to the dictators until war had made it
unavoidable. The problems and personalities of the late

forties and beyond were, naturally enough, entirely different and new in style. The built-in acknowledgment by the British people that the Tory chiefs were the anointed and appointed leaders of the people had vanished, at any rate for a time. If by some accident Churchill, Eden and their friends had been returned to power in 1945 we might well have had a very un-English bloody revolution in our country. Instead we got Attlee, Morrison, Bevin and so on. Perhaps we may ruminate, seeing Britain's position today, that a little blood-letting might have been no bad thing, as once or twice further back in our history. But that is a complicated speculation.

As deputy leader of the Opposition Eden had to take a general oversight of domestic as well as foreign problems. He was not well qualified to deal with the former and he knew it. He was apt to speak of the ideal of 'a property-owning democracy' as if it meant something significant. This opaque phrase had been employed by a Tory colleague as far back as the 1920s and it entirely lacked electorate appeal. In Britain, after all, practically everyone owns property and practically everyone is democratic. Even a comparatively simple-minded elector wishes to know: how much property in each case, and how is it going to be redistributed so that there's more for me? On this the Tories were silent, except to say that as soon as the various controls, which were essential just after the war, had been removed everything would come right for everybody.

Eden and his successor as Foreign Secretary, Ernest Bevin, were of course as dissimilar in most ways as they could possibly be. They had however worked well enough together in the War Cabinet and had some regard for each other. In two ways they were similar. They were both personally vain. Lord Moran puts it rather roughly: 'Bevin talked about himself – non-stop, as they say – while Eden, a vainer man, learnt reticence.' Secondly, while the spectacle of the lumbering great Ernie was something unparalleled in the FO and he announced at the start that

86

he was going to run things his way, the charm, tradition and so on of the officials, their manners and their methods soon won him over. In the first debate in the House after the formation of the Labour government Eden said that there had never been a serious difference of opinion on foreign affairs between Labour and Conservative ministers in the War Cabinet, and Bevin confirmed this. The chief reason had been that Churchill had, except on rare occasions, dominated the scene. What was now needed, in our diplomacy quite as much as in our domestic policy, was a radical change. It did not come about. Bevin may have been more realistic about the necessity for some changes in our posture world-wide than Eden would have been at that stage. But only marginally. In most directions our professional diplomats saw to it that the dynamism and the forward-looking attitudes were suavely side-tracked. They would speak of and approach the problems of Europe and Asia as if they remained much as before the war. But they had changed cataclysmically.

Eden gives practically no space in his memoirs to the years in opposition. They did not represent an effective part of his life. His health had been shaken by the war and in any case he did not enjoy his role. At times he criticised the government for going too fast in shedding the empire. But most of the time he could not even disagree strongly with their foreign policy.

Inside the FO Bevin duly put into practice the 'Eden' reforms, which were by no means as radical as Eden himself thought. A proportion of the bright and energetic outsiders who had joined the FO in the war remained on; Sir Patrick Dean, for instance, has gone right to the top. But on the whole business was conducted much as before. Although work officially began at 9.30 a m, rather than 11 as before the war, few officials of any seniority cranked up before 10. Skeleton staffs were even maintained, for skeleton hours, at weekends. In 1946 Sir Alexander Cadogan, who had been head of the Office since 1938, was sent as our first ambassador to the United Nations. He was already sixty-two and a purely traditional type of diplomat. A younger and more original man would have been better. He was succeeded as Permanent Under-Secretary by Sir Orme ('Moley') Sargent, a man with a sardonic wit who had hardly ever served abroad. Although a conventional diplomat by career and in his manner, he was capable of constructive ideas. Immensely tall and thin, he got on very well with the gargantuan Bevin. They carried out a combined operation to take over the Commonwealth Relations Office; but the minister, Philip Noel-Baker, and his officials thwarted this sensible scheme.

The fundamental lines which our diplomacy was to follow, and which Eden was to take over on his return to the FO in 1951, soon became clear. In August 1945 the US exercised her nuclear power and ended the war in the Far East. In the same month she exercised her economic power when President Truman ordered the cessation of lend-lease as he was in duty bound to do. Within a couple of months a pattern now all too familiar to us today was established: a British mission went off to Washington to beg for a loan, which was granted on fairly stiff conditions. They would have been worse but for the unconventional and adroit diplomacy of the economist Maynard Keynes on our side. In September the allied Foreign Ministers met in London for the first of an endless series of discussions over the years about Germany. Preposterous conditions, known by each side to be unacceptable to the others, were regularly put forward in turn. Our diplomats' attitude was that since a united German had existed, even if only for a comparatively short time in history, it had the right to exist again. The Communists on the other hand, judging that united Germany on its appalling record, were even more determined that it should not revive. These conferences seemed designed to exacerbate relations between the Western allies and the USSR. Eden joined readily in the game when he returned to power. In the same month another problem that would give Eden trouble enough cast its long shadow before: Egypt demanded the revision of

88

the Anglo-Egyptian treaty of 1936, the end of military occupation which that treaty had stipulated, and Egyptian sovereignty over the Sudan, at that time officially an Anglo-Egyptian condominium but in practice a British colony.

The United Nations creaked into action with some fifty members. HMG were not sure quite how seriously to take it. It was hoped that it would preserve peace; but since the major powers were bitterly divided amongst themselves this smacked of over-optimism. In March 1946 Churchill, who in opposition as when in power was more rumbustious than Eden, made the speech at Fulton, Missouri, which gave world-wide currency to the image of 'the iron curtain' that had come down across the middle of Europe. Communism made a significant advance westwards – its last one – when Gottwald became premier of Czechoslovakia in May. The final Communist takeover followed in February 1948. In April 1946 the League of Nations assembly had solemnly dissolved itself. At least that absurd relic of the 1930s was out of the way. At the Nuremberg trials some other pernicious relics were dealt with.

In 1947 the US's supremacy in the West, which many of our diplomats and politicians found it difficult to acknowledge, was further emphasised in two major connexions. The Truman doctrine of economic and military aid to states considered to be threatened by Communism was announced. Its first applications were made to the cases of Greece and Turkey. Traditionally these countries, and the rest of the Middle East, had been a part of the world where British experience and expertise were assumed to be dominant. Just as Eden always thought and said that the Americans could not understand Europe, so they were supposed not to understand the Middle East. But having saved Greece from Communism in 1944 by a much criticised military intervention, we now had to admit that we just could not afford financially to keep her or Turkey safe. That was revolutionary enough. But there was more to it than that. The US Foreign Service had up till this period tended to look up to our Diplomatic Service and, full of able people though it was, to defer in the most courteous manner to our experience, training and methods. I had found this to be the case even at a junior level. Further, the Central Intelligence Agency, today as powerful as the US Foreign Service, had just been formed with the help of much advice from the British Secret Intelligence Service including that of the as yet undetected traitor Philby. The Truman doctrine was a turning point for these two powerful services. The British apron-strings were severed. We took a long time – until after Eden's fall – to realise that in diplomacy as in more fundamental things the young American giant was out on his own and was in no way a servant of British interests.

The other great US initiative was the call by ex-General, now Secretary of State, George Marshall for a European Recovery Programme, which came to be known as Marshall Aid. This imaginative and generous proposal offered large quantities of dollar help to any European countries which would help themselves. Bevin rightly jumped at it. All the other West European countries welcomed it. Czechoslovakia nibbled and was slapped down by the USSR who decreed that the Communist East could and should do without. Marshall Aid rescued Western Europe from economic chaos.

This was one wise act by Bevin and the government of the day. Another in 1947 was the hustling through of independence for India and Pakistan, achieved under the aegis of Lord Mountbatten at the cost of perhaps a million lives thrown away in the final partition struggles. No one could say today that either state is a very satisfactory entity, India in particular. But the time had come and we were well rid of the burden. Burma became independent in January 1948. All these developments caused much pain and grief to Churchill, Eden and most of their Conservative colleagues.

Nineteen-forty-eight was a crucial year for Europe. The USSR still did not possess her own nuclear weapon; and Marshall Aid was clearly going to emphasise the economic inferiority of the Communist countries. In particular it would serve to pull up West Germany, with all the dangers that implied, while East Germany was still held down in the military, economic and political grip which the Soviet government and its German supporters under Ulbricht considered necessary. After the Communist *coup d'état* in Czechoslovakia in February came the Soviet walkout of the quadripartite Control Commission for Germany in March. (The photograph of the Soviet general who walked out was still preserved in the Commission's Berlin committee room when I was British minister there in 1962, and no doubt still is, supposedly as a sign that quadrilateral collaboration still existed.) The Soviet authorities then began to interfere with access to West Berlin and, after the reform of West German currency in June had underlined the difference in the rates of economic progress of the two parts of Germany, they instituted the Berlin blockade in July. In the face of all this extreme Soviet toughness Britain, France and Benelux in March signed the Brussels Treaty of alliance for fifty years in the economic and military spheres – a sort of mini-NATO. As with NATO France has rather curtailed its effectiveness. In June the Brussels Treaty powers plus the US called for the first steps towards the independence of West Germany. And as soon as the Berlin blockade was instituted Bevin and his colleagues thought up an immediate riposte: the airlift which kept Berlin going and finally broke the blockade in the following May. In Berlin today the major credit is given to the US air forces, and rightly. The initiative however was Bevin's, and he was backed by Churchill and Eden. An adroit move of Bevin's at this point was to send the Oxford don Sir Oliver Franks as ambassador to Washington instead of the next man on the official precedence list. Though reserved in manner he hit it off well with the Americans and deployed his sharp brain to good effect over the next four and a half years. In 1948, too, Israel was born with blood and slaughter which have not ceased twenty years later.

In April 1949 NATO came into being and guaranteed for at least twenty years the participation of the US and Canada in the defence and development of Western Europe. (It was intended to guarantee that of France too, but under de Gaulle she has gone rogue.) The so-called Council of Europe, which in fact contained only non-Communist countries, was set up at Strasbourg. Bevin, and for that matter Eden, never took seriously this timid attempt at a European get-together. Churchill was more forthcoming and farseeing, not least because he realised that the Americans were in earnest when they pressed for an integrated Western Europe including Britain. The Russians gave in over the Berlin blockade; and no sooner had the Federal Republic of Germany come into being than they created the German Democratic Republic. The policy of pushing ahead with West Germany's independence and development was bi-partisan in Britain. Sometimes we failed to realise to what extent it was bound to stiffen the Soviet government's German policy and the iron curtain. Two further events were even more portentous for the future. The People's Republic of China was proclaimed by Mao Tse-tung and Chou En-lai. We hastened to recognise it, as realism demanded, but this annoyed the Americans and moreover received scant thanks in the next twenty years from the Chinese Communists. Finally the Soviet Union exploded her first atomic bomb. But she felt no cause for complacency or relaxation, for the US was by now well stocked with A bombs and hot on the trail of the hydrogen bomb, with the Soviet Union breathing down her neck.

The last years of the Labour government, 1950 and 1951, were also the years of the spies. The Rosenbergs, Klaus Fuchs and others were caught; Maclean and Burgess got away; Philby was very nearly caught but got away with it. All such people, and others who would be detected later on, were supplying invaluable nuclear, military, political and other intelligence to the Communists. Thus at a critical moment in the Korean war, which the North Koreans began in June 1950, Maclean was able to assure the Communists from his top-secret knowledge of the US government's policy that they would not use nuclear weapons or invade China if China came to the help of North Korea. She accordingly did so, in a massive way. In Europe Churchill carried at Strasbourg a motion in favour of a European army, and NATO discussed the formation of an integrated defence force. In April 1951 the Six took the first solid step towards the Common Market when they signed the Paris treaty setting up a single coal and steel authority. We had watched the negotiations going on but had not seriously tried to participate. Marshall Aid to Britain was terminated. Without it we should have been in a fearful mess. But even with it the British economy was not developing as well as the West German, French and others. In Communist Europe Poland and East Germany agreed that the existing Oder-Neisse line should be their permanent frontier. In the Middle East Musaddiq chased the British oil concerns out of Iran; and on 27th October 1951, the very day when Churchill formed his government, Egypt abrogated the 1936 treaty of alliance with Britain and the 1899 agreement on the Sudan.

All in all, Britain's posture in the world was equivocal. The economic base was unsatisfactory. We had rightly divested ourselves of some political commitments; but we still attempted to exert influence all over the place, and our forces were distributed across the world. Having handed over our atomic secrets to the US for the purpose of winning the war we now had to work painfully on our own towards making our first nuclear weapon. If our posture was to be improved in fact, as distinct from illusorily, some profound changes would have to be made at the base and these would have to be backed by a new, tough, realistic diplomacy everywhere. The question was, could the old firm of Churchill and Eden achieve all this?

NINE

The Old Firm

THEY NEVER HAD a hope, in point of fact. The country was fed up with the restrictions imposed by Labour, necessary though they had been. I remember vividly the contrast between the *dolce vita* of our life at the embassy in Chile from 1948 and the return to Britain in 1951. On the boat we learnt of the defection of Maclean and Burgess and thought it either incredible or some sort of macabre joke. Back in London we found we had to manage with one egg per person per week and 1s 3d worth of meat. The foreign travel allowance varied between nil and twenty-five pounds per year. People began to ask whether we had won the war, and if so to what purpose?

So Churchill and Eden were welcomed back, though the overall Conservative majority was under twenty. Churchill was now a really old man of seventy-seven. Lord Moran calls his memoirs of him *The Struggle for Survival* and even dates that struggle back to 1940. Churchill's extraordinary physique and resilience had enabled him to survive coronaries and strokes that would have despatched a lesser man on several occasions. But naturally enough his speed of working and of thought was impaired. Eden was only fifty-four but his health had suffered more than was at first apparent as a result of wartime strain and peacetime boredom. It was ten years since he had been promised the succession, and the question hung in the air between the two men. Eden was happy to return to the FO, of course; but he would have been happier to go to Number Ten. They both became increasingly difficult to work with. Churchill combined bursts of energy and demands which seemed less appropriate than in wartime with periods of lethargy. Eden was conscientious as ever, but more and more tetchy. For instance, during their joint visit to President Truman and Secretary of State Acheson in January 1952 an undignified wrangle took place. Eden complained that the draft communiqué referred constantly to the Prime Minister and his instructions to the Foreign Secretary. 'No one instructs me,' he maintained. He redrafted the communiqué to make the point; Churchill refused to accept the redraft.

Neither man had the slightest idea how to 'set the people free', as the slogan was, and bring Britain to economic prosperity at the same time. A 'bonfire of controls' had political appeal but could not of itself restore our standing in the world. The decisive diplomatic style of wartime, which Churchill had deployed effectively, no longer applied. Eden was faced with distasteful behaviour by the United Nations and its various members, many of them with black, brown or yellow skins and formerly known to him only as people with whom the Dominions and Colonial Offices had dealings. As usual, too, he had difficulties with our allies. The Americans were now unquestionably very powerful. The French did not seem to look towards us quite as before. The Russians were our enemies in the Cold War. They could still be lectured, but it made no impact. Eden called the volume of his memoirs which deals with this period, and which he wrote soon after his retirement, *Full Circle*. An apt title so far as his conduct of affairs was concerned. Unfortunately for him, history neither repeats itself nor moves in circles.

One of Eden's first actions set the tone of his diplomacy from now on. Predictably, it concerned Egypt. He sent a stiffish note to the Egyptian government stating that, whatever they might care to say about the 1899 and 1936 agreements, we intended to stick to our treaty rights. He made two very different comments on this matter. First he observed, fairly enough though not publicly at the time, that the 1936 treaty did not give us the right to maintain large forces in

Egypt. When I was in our Cairo embassy in 1946 and 1947 I had seen how much the Egyptians detested our military presence, not least when a crowd succeeded in burning four soldiers to death in an Alexandria square. As for Maclean, who followed me, it was the corruptly colonial atmosphere of Egypt which finally sent him round the bend. But Eden also went on to say that if we did not maintain our treaty rights, including non-existent rights, 'no reliance could be placed on any international agreement and the whole structure and basis of international relations would cease to exist. This was consistently applied by us to later events.' To be fair on these hysterical statements they were written in the heat of the moment shortly after his Suez disaster. But they show what was in his mind. He had no idea that in the 1950s events were moving several times faster than in the 1930s. He had no realisation that treaties and agreements were liable to need revision every ten years at least, rather than every twenty or sixty. In a word, he had no idea that 'the whole structure and basis of international relations' had changed, like other things. It was this blind unawareness that was to lead him eventually to commit aggression in what he imagined was a just cause and in such a way as to earn the obloquy of the world. Our senior diplomats did little to modify these attitudes.

Anglo-Egyptian relations did not develop well and for this Eden blamed not only the Egyptians but also the Americans. He told the Egyptian government, hectoringly, that incidents must cease and that there could be no question of evacuating British forces. He explained to the US government the difficulties which would be posed by a withdrawal while we were preparing for the defence of the Middle East against external aggression. It went without saying that he was referring to the Soviet Union. But anyone knowing the Soviet mentality could have told him that the Soviet government would never act in that way at a distance from their military base. Subversion yes, by all and every means; and in this connexion the presence of our garrison positively helped the Soviet cause. Eden got little sympathy from the US government or, in particular, the US ambassador in Cairo. He expected them to join us in exerting pressure on Egypt. For two good reasons they had no intention of doing so. First, it was repugnant to them to help maintain a colonial-type policy whose legal base was anyway rocky. Secondly, their interests in the Middle East were different from ours; for a start they were much less involved commercially. Eden and the FO never grasped these points, right up to the end. He also complained that the US government were unwilling to take second place in an area where 'primary responsibility' was not theirs. Responsibility for what? As the Americans saw it, we were trying to perpetuate outdated responsibilities at the cost of various nations who should be encouraged to look after themselves. Eden finds another scapegoat in fat, self-indulgent King Farouk. A course at Woolwich might have put some stuffing into him, he says. From my acquaintance with His Majesty I have my doubts on this. He was incorrigible. Over the Sudan question, where equally the US government disagreed with our methods, Eden even differed from Churchill – 'one of the rare occasions', he comments. But on the treaty negotiations he has to admit that if Egypt were to invoke international authority the verdict was likely to be against us. A bit difficult to square this with respect for the sanctity of treaties, and so on.

However he was back on this vague and general line when reflecting broadly on the Middle East and Africa. He wanted to encourage national aspirations but not to 'indulge uncontrolled appetites'. Black, brown and other leaders should at all times behave like members of the English upper class. In practice he showed little sympathy with them. He never bothered to visit Black Africa. He complained that there was a tendency to favour the developing nations and apply different standards when it came to those who were already developed. What is surprising is that anyone should expect anything else. It is, after all, the developing nations who need the help. Eden had loved the League of Nations, where a comparatively small and developed group of powers could discuss to their hearts' content schemes for preserving the peace which looked good on paper, even if they were useless in practice. But as the United Nations became steadily larger and rougher, and less and less inclined to respect traditional British interests and Pax Britannica, Eden came to dislike it more and more. So that finally he decided to flout it entirely; and that was the end for him.

The most important development in 1952, for diplomacy as for life in general, was the explosion by the US of the world's first H bomb in November. The USSR followed suit nine months later. The escalation so well analysed later by Herman Kahn was in full spate. Britain came tagging along with her first A bomb in February and proceeded down the H bomb trail. I was involved inside the FO in all our politico-strategic matters from 1952 to 1958. It seemed to me that one or two of our military leaders – not many – had some conception of what was cooking and how to deal with it. Amongst our political leaders very few grasped the implications for diplomacy and strategy. Eden was uneasy with such problems. It would have required a Churchill at his best to weigh the totally new considerations and adapt our policy accordingly. Unfortunately we did not possess a figure of that calibre. As for our professional diplomats they preferred almost to a man to regard all questions arising from going over to 'nukes' as outside their province.

Inside Europe, however, there were matters which appeared, though delusively, to be susceptible to the old Eden treatment of minutes, *notes verbales*, *aide-mémoires* and so on. What he calls frivolously, but in a sense justifiably, the battle of the notes over Germany got into full swing. In March 1952 the Soviet government proposed a four-power conference on questions affecting the reunification and rearmament of the two parts of Germany. The head of the FO at this time, Sir William Strang, and his two successors, Sir Ivone Kirkpatrick and Sir Frederick Hoyer Millar, were all 'German experts' and did nothing to distract Eden from the Adenauer-influenced view of the German problem which he was constitutionally inclined to adopt. Adenauer was to become one of his few close friends and one of the very few diplomatic colleagues, whether British or foreign, whom he seldom criticised. Consequently Eden's analysis of the situation was biased and unrealistic, and therefore unproductive as regards any possibilities of progress on the problem. He considered the Soviet position on East Germany to be equivocal; whereas it was firm and clear. He thought that they dared not offer to end the division of Germany in the only way which could attract West German opinion, namely by free elections. In fact they had no wish to end the division or to attract West German opinion, and they had their suspicions of those 'free elections'.

In reply to their note, therefore, Eden and his allies stated that discussions of a German peace treaty could only follow the creation of an all-German government by free elections supervised by a United Nations Commission which had previously satisfied itself that in 'the Soviet zone', or more accurately the German Democratic Republic, as well as in Berlin and the Federal Republic adequate safeguards existed for the liberties of the individual. It was assumed that the United Nations Commission would give the right answer on West Germany, though annoyingly for Eden such commissions on similar problems, for instance in the Middle East, did not always toe the Eden line. Thus the Western powers put this enormous cart before the horse. Now in diplomacy the method of rearranging vehicle and animal priorities is a perfectly permissible one so long as you know what you are doing, which in this case was to make all profitable negotiation impossible. What is nugatory is to convince yourself that you are making a worthwhile contribution to negotiation when you are not. Eden complained that after this exchange the Soviet government's notes became increasingly uncompromising; into the bargain he seemed surprised at this. He insisted that the West's conditions for reunification were practical, unlike the Communists'.

Well, they have not led to any practical developments over sixteen years later. He went on about the discredited Soviet zone régime. Well, Ulbricht and his government are more firmly in power in 1968 than then. For years our embassy in Bonn and commandant in Berlin reported that Ulbricht was on the point of disappearing because he was such a nasty man. To this I replied repeatedly, both before my time as minister in Berlin in 1961–2, during it, and since on two lines: first, Ulbricht and the Communists no doubt enjoyed being nasty and provocative to the West and would continue the process so long as it was successful from their point of view. Secondly, if our diplomats repeated their reports for long enough they would be proved correct; for even Ulbricht was subject to nature in the end.

It is proving a long haul for our prophets and Ulbricht at seventy-five seems sprier than most of his contemporaries. Eden followed up these criticisms with the pronouncement that we could not compromise on our principles or on any Soviet proposals aiming at German neutralisation. 'It was not, after all, our fault if the result of freedom of choice would be to align Germany with us.' Lord Avon has never, of course, visited the German Democratic Republic as I have. I can assure him that today there are none too many of its citizens who would like to align themselves with the Western alliance which includes the Americans with their Vietnam activities, and the Federal Republic with its toleration of the new Nazis. A final comment in Eden's grandest manner: 'The need to keep [sic] Europe united remains an imperative for statesmanship to realise.'

In May 1952 the European Defence Community treaty was signed in Paris, with reciprocal NATO-EDC guarantees. This was a sincere attempt at West European integration, encouraged by the US but doomed to failure when it came to the question of ratification by its signatories. Bevin had held aloof from these efforts and Eden was with him. When the French Foreign Minister said that the UK would at some later date again be formally invited to join Eden's reflexion was that it was embarrassing to be forced, as he put it, to say no by the forthcoming attitude of our allies. This sort of attitude was naturally not forgotten by our West European friends, and particularly the French, when we later made signs of wanting to join the Common Market. All such questions of Britain integrating herself in West European bodies were handled with not only traditional reserve by our diplomats but with a lack of seriousness. The attitude was that we were still the impregnable island centre of a great empire, enjoying our special relationship with the US, and these curious new bodies in Europe must wait. And thus we missed a whole series of buses.

In July 1952 General Neguib seized power in Egypt and removed the flaccid Farouk. He is partly of Sudanese origin, and it proved possible to come to a sensible agreement with him and his government, including Nasser, over the next few months. This was an opportunity for us to adopt a more modern line in our policy to Egypt. We could have got on friendly terms with Neguib and Nasser if we had changed the tone of our diplomacy. But under Churchill, Eden and our traditional diplomats this was not on. Eden soon added Nasser to the list of his foes; and here was another vendetta in which Eden was to be worsted.

Eisenhower was elected President in November 1952 and without delay Eden asked him not to select John Foster Dulles as his Secretary of State. Eden and Foster Dulles had met several times and could not get on together at all. Dulles was a difficult man in some ways but he was also a very shrewd one who knew from personal involvement the wide world outside politics. Eden's whole manner and style grated on him, and vice versa. Eisenhower naturally paid no attention to Eden's intervention and, being the co-ordinator and delegator of authority that he was, made Dulles not only Secretary of State but an unusually powerful one. He was certainly too much for Eden, who later on referred to him publicly as 'that terrible man'. After a tour of the Middle East early in 1953 Dulles gave fair warning of what the US government's policy there would be. He called Neguib 'one of the outstanding Free World leaders of the post-war period'. He also made it clear that the US had no intention of supporting the old colonial interests of Britain and France. Eden preferred to ignore the warning and to assume that the 'special relationship' would prevail in every crisis.

Churchill showed bursts of his old energy in 1953. As soon as his old friend Eisenhower was installed in January he paid him a visit and all was cordiality. In March, just too soon to witness the explosion of the first Soviet H bomb, Stalin died, and was succeeded by the comparatively unknown Malenkov. Churchill, without consulting Eden, the FO, our ambassador in Moscow or anyone else, at once came out in favour of 'a meeting at the summit'. Eisenhower was doubtful; Eden was piqued. The FO said that long preparation would be necessary. It is possible that if Churchill's proposal had been swiftly followed up something might have been achieved, as so much had been at the wartime meetings of the Big Three. But the weight of inertia was too much, Churchill's health had a relapse, his idea was not realised for many months and it proved a flop in the changed circumstances.

Confirmation of the Soviet government's determination to remain absolutely firm on East Germany was provided in June. A rising against Ulbricht's government which began in East Berlin and spread to parts of the provinces was crushed without difficulty by the Red Army. Stalin's policies were clearly not going to be swept away in a day. Nevertheless Britain proposed another four-power conference on Germany and after the usual complications over the agenda this came off in Berlin in January and February 1954. Meanwhile Khrushchev had mounted another rung of the ladder by becoming First Secretary of the Central Committee of the USSR Communist Party.

The run-up to Eden's good year of 1954 was not all that promising. At the Bermuda meeting of Eisenhower, Churchill and Laniel (a name that rings no bell today), together with their Foreign Ministers, it became apparent that France was wavering on the EDC and that Britain was no help in that direction either. Dulles told the Press that if France failed to ratify then the US government would have to undertake an 'agonising reappraisal' of its policy. He told Eden that the US and Britain might well be reaching a parting of the ways. The US might swing over to a policy of western hemispheric defence with the emphasis on the Far East. Eden reflected that his relations with the four earlier American Secretaries of State whom he had known as colleagues had been 'always cordial and often intimate'. But with Dulles he found it difficult to make out what he really meant. While granting that allies should subordinate their interests to some extent in accordance with their stronger partner's thinking he could not see that an alliance could flourish on that basis. But is there in fact any other sound basis? I do not mean that we should kowtow to our American friends. But we ought to have worked out years ago a realistic basis for our relationship in which appreciation of their all-round strength, and of their considerate handling of many of our problems, was given due weight. In this way the balance might have been better kept to this day.

TEN

A Good Year?

THUS THE OMENS for 1954 were mixed, but Eden was fully
into his stride by now. It seemed like the 1930s. Meeting
followed meeting, first inside the FO and then abroad, on
every conceivable subject. The FO's two top men, Sir
William Strang and Sir Ivone Kirkpatrick, played along
readily in their different ways. Strang was the complete
bureaucrat whose skill lay not in suggesting new ideas but in
serving up situation reports in palatable form to ministers.
He was one of only two senior members of the FO who had
not been to public school and Oxbridge, and was constantly
exhibited like a prize heifer as a proof of our profound
democracy. True, at six inches' distance you could not tell
the difference between him and an Old Wykehamist. Kirkpatrick was more original. A Roman Catholic, he had concerned himself with propaganda in both World Wars.
He produced and welcomed enterprising ideas, but was
perfectly happy to abandon them if they would not work.
He took the Suez affair in his stride; he even showed zest
for it. Both Strang and Kirkpatrick had been at the head of
our affairs in West Germany and both were intent on building up her strength. Like Eden, they were admirers of
Adenauer. It is just about unique that Eden never has a harsh
or even narking word to say about him.

So throughout 1953 and 1954 the 'Eden plans' rolled off
the drawing-board and were tested out in the international
forum. As in the 1930s the fact of having produced a
plan, however impracticable, was considered a useful bit
of diplomacy in itself. Sometimes, when the producers

brought forth a time-wasting plan with their tongues in their cheeks, this might be so. But all too many of these plans were liable to make the Communists more stubborn, and sometimes offend our allies into the bargain. These international conferences tended to resemble some intricate formal dance.

Eden began the Berlin conference on 25th January with some optimism. He thought Molotov showed signs of friendliness 'and so I am asking a small party of bears to dinner'. Back in the zoo again. Molotov seemed to Eden to be interested in his plan for the security of all countries – that smacks of 'collective security' in the 1930s – including the USSR. This was a clever bit of deception by Molotov. First, the USSR would never rely on anyone else for her security. Secondly, she now had the A bomb and the H bomb and was perfectly capable of looking after herself. Whenever Eden sounded off about free elections, Molotov repeated 'the familiar Soviet themes'. That made two playing the same game. He reminded Eden that Hitler had come to power through free elections. When Eden pointed out that if, despite the safeguards of the European Defence Community, Germany were to attack the USSR we should be at the latter's side in accordance with the Anglo-Soviet treaty, Molotov expressed scepticism, and well he might. The EDC did not exist, for a start. If it were to come into being it was evidently not going to provide reliable safeguards. Molotov pointed out, justifiably, that it was directed against the USSR, and that Adenauer was an enemy of his country. He asked that all should combine to prevent effectively any revival of German militarism. Eden persisted. His object was to persuade Molotov that the Western allies had not come to Berlin merely to oppose the USSR. In this he failed. When Molotov proposed that representatives of both the Federal and Democratic Republics should be invited to attend, Dulles as chairman turned him down flat. Eden put the Western plan in detail and this, he recollects with modest pride, became known as 'the Eden plan'. It was one of many

106

so called. The net result was that western policy was now 'on record for all to see'.

There was no other result. Molotov simply ignored the plan for five sessions and then rejected it brusquely. He saw in Western ideas for reunification a device for turning the whole of Germany into an ally against the USSR. In spite of protestations by Eden and his friends he was dead right, of course. The Western allies were asking the USSR to give up all the advantages of her position in Germany in return for nothing at all. Eden tried hard to show why Germany could never again resort to aggression. I think he even believed it. Diplomacy has reached a pretty pass when you deceive yourself. Eden says, without humour, that the only worthwhile result of the Berlin conference was to lead on to another one – the Geneva conference on the totally different subject of the Far East. When reporting to the House he was at pains to scotch the 'deceptively attractive solution' of neutralising Germany. It certainly appealed to a number of people in this country and elsewhere and still does today. The Soviet government had the last word this time round when, with a rare flash of humour, they offered to join NATO. You have to laugh. Yet diplomacy could do with some bursts of inspiration from time to time, however far out they may seem. Perhaps this was one. Perhaps an even greater one was the suggestion made at the end of the war by Bernard Baruch, the highly respected unofficial adviser of the President and lifelong friend of Churchill, that the US government should voluntarily share its then unique nuclear secrets with the Soviet government. Of course the politicians and diplomats stamped on that one. Yet it is worth a little speculation whether such a daring initiative might not have taken the heat out of the terrible nuclear rivalry which has continued ever since, and is now more dangerous than ever.

The Geneva conference, which opened on 26th April and lasted, off and on, nearly three months, was high drama throughout. Chou En-lai attended, for the first and last time so far as a conference of this type was concerned. His North

Korean advisers were in the same case. When the conference opened Dien Bien Phu was falling to the North Vietnamese and the Americans wanted to save the French garrison by a massive air intervention. It fell on 6th May. Eden was in his element as a negotiator, his favourite role. He enjoyed operating again, as in the 1930s, in the Palais des Nations, staying in the familiar Hôtel Beau Rivage, and even seeing pictures of himself when young in some of the cafés. Afterwards he stated categorically that the restoration of peace in Indo-China was the most dangerous and acute problem he faced during those years as Foreign Secretary. All the same some of his actions were heavy-handed. The problem, as he expressed it to the Prime Minister in a telegram, was to please the bear (again) without parting us from the eagle. What about the dragon? He had discussions with Chou En-lai and obviously felt at sea with him. He managed to annoy the French and, fatally, Foster Dulles. Protesting that he had been a Francophile all his life – and with his supreme betrayal of them over Suez yet to come – he lectured their Minister of Defence, Pleven, at this tragic moment on how France should increase her period of National Service. A preliminary message to Dulles, which Eden quotes with satisfaction, was downright rude: 'Americans may think the time past when they need consider the feelings or difficulties of their allies. It is the conviction that this tendency becomes more pronounced every week that is creating mounting difficulties for anyone in this country who wants to maintain close Anglo-American relations.' Eden discouraged all Dulles' suggestions for intervention over Dien Bien Phu, and he was no doubt right on this. But the result of it all was that Dulles lost his temper and refused to work any more with Eden.

As soon as the conference began Dulles sent for his Under-Secretary, Bedell Smith, and handed over to him on 1st May. The Communists must have been laughing up their capacious sleeves. Eden was relieved, but on the day before Dulles quit there was an acrimonious discussion. Dulles accused the British of dragging their feet for months over the question of helping the French. He said that the Western allies were in complete disarray. He then stormed off back to Washington in a dudgeon. Eden found consolation in his relations with Molotov, who was happy to drive a wedge here and there. This apart, however, Eden and Molotov together contributed much to overcoming French reluctance, American apprehension and Chinese suspicion. This was, he comments, the first international conference at which he was sharply conscious of the deterrent effect of the H bomb on both sides. Anyway, the conference arranged for the war to end and it laid down the conditions in which four small successor states to Indo-China should exist.

This was indeed something, and Eden's negotiating skill had proved considerable. But as on so many occasions he and the FO tended to conclude that, thanks to the pieces of paper signed right and left, a solid new situation had been created. On the contrary, it has proved catastrophically liquid. Laos and Cambodia are surviving, under constant threat, by the skin of their teeth. I need not enlarge on the position in and between North and South Vietnam. Eden from the sidelines, and our various Foreign Secretaries from Whitehall, nowadays continually appeal to their 'fellow-chairman' of 1954, the Soviet Foreign Minister, to help. He continually replies with a *nyet*. 1968 is not 1954. The Communists have manœuvred the Americans into a terrible, even disgraceful, position. They are not going to rescue them for the sake of agreements that are fourteen years old. It is not Eden's fault that his 'victory' at Geneva has turned hollow. But it is no good his suggesting remedies, as he does from time to time, which are based on out-of-date premises. And the cost of his 'victory', even at the time, was resentment on the part of the French, which they bore with admirable equanimity – until the time for de Gaulle's revenge came. It was also bitter alienation on the part of the US government which manifested itself powerfully in a shorter period, only two years later, over Suez. Equally grave was the fact that

Eden and his diplomats were not aware of the full force of the feeling they had aroused in our closest allies. A negotiation had been 'successfully' concluded, and that was that.

Edən managed to offend his allies further over the negotiations for the South-East Asia Treaty Organisation which was designed as an anti-Communist counter to the concessions that had to be made on Indo-China. He had suggested a 'Locarno-type' defensive agreement and thus raised a storm of outraged protest in the US where Locarno, not unnaturally, was associated with the bad old days. Eden was, amazingly, amazed. All he had meant was a get-together of anti-Communist powers in South-East Asia to discuss the planning of defensive measures against certain contingencies. But in quoting Locarno he had overlooked so many things. First, it was old hat: half of his colleagues had to look up the textbooks of the 1920s and 1930s quickly to make sure of what he was on about. Secondly, there was no parallel at all between Locarno of the 1920s and SEATO of the 1950s. Thirdly, Americans associated it with appeasement. Finally, Locarno had been a flop. However, in September the US, Britain, France, Australia, New Zealand, Pakistan, Thailand and the Philippines signed a treaty; it was purely consultative and had no teeth in it. In fact it had, and has today, less significance than the ANZUS pact signed in 1951 between the US, Australia and New Zealand with Britain excluded. Never mind; another treaty under the belt.

Meanwhile, in June, Churchill had paid another visit to Eisenhower in Washington with the object of patching up relations and this, in the style of the wartime visits, had resulted in a sweeping declaration of Western policy known as the Potomac Charter. No one remembers it today. It bore other resemblances to the wartime meetings as well. Our ambassador Sir Roger Makins had for some time tried to persuade Eden that from our point of view Dulles was a good Secretary of State. Churchill told him that Dulles wanted to be friendly. The President himself tried to blunt the sharp differences between Dulles and Eden. Churchill eventually got angry with Eden for choosing this occasion to quarrel once more with Dulles and asked him whether he did not realise the extent to which Britain depended on the US. To no avail. Churchill, American himself on his mother's side, was always ready to do the leg-work in order to meet the US President of the day and never insisted that one of them should come to Britain for discussion. Nor did Attlee. Eden was more grudging about this state of affairs until it was too late.

In August 1954, when Churchill temporarily took over the FO during Eden's absence through illness, he remarked unkindly to Lord Moran: 'It is a great relief to have charge of the FO instead of having to argue with Anthony. He is most conscientious, plugging away at a routine. But that's not what's wanted at the FO, where you must take up the big issues and deal with them.'

The next Western moves on Germany were presented in a high-minded fashion and the Western governments did not appreciate the extent to which they solidified the division of Europe. Churchill and Eden, and their allies, considered that the Federal Republic's sovereignty must be 'restored'. She had, of course, never been sovereign. She must be free to form the alliances of her choice. Eden comments that the Russians would try to tempt Germany away from the West and that this must be countered. This loose talk about 'Germany' and 'Europe' has bedevilled our diplomacy ever since the war and continues to do so today. If you base your diplomacy on inaccurate thoughts, such as that Western Germany is 'Germany' and Western Europe is 'Europe', the end-product is bound to be unsatisfactory. On this occasion the US and Britain made the running and Adenauer responded graciously: he would accept safeguards, that is against his own country going aggressive once more, so long as they did not 'discriminate against Germany'. The meaning is opaque, but Eden saw statesmanship in this reaction. He proposed that the Brussels Treaty should be transformed into a mutual defence pact 'of the Locarno type'. There we have the harking back once more. The advantage it possessed over NATO, he argued, was that it lasted (not would last) fifty years as against twenty. This was the apotheosis of the belief in a signed piece of paper as the '*Ding an sich*'. Dulles at this point flew to see Adenauer without consulting Eden, which offended him, and told him not to fiddle about with the Brussels Treaty but to get ready to join NATO. Adenauer of course agreed, after a little quiet blackmail on the lines that German (*ie* West German) youth must be saved from any temptation to go Nazi again. We can send up an earnest prayer on that today. Eden had what he considered a most satisfactory visit to Bonn during which his personal relations with Adenauer were excellent. He then lectured the French Prime Minister Mendès-France on the dangers of his negative policy which would drive Germany [*sic*] into the arms of Russia [*sic*] and the US into 'fortress America'. In this he was, no doubt unwittingly, acting as the mouthpiece of his not very close friend Dulles, and also showing the extent to which he was under the Adenauer spell.

October 1954 was momentous. A nine-power conference in London on what was broadly called European unity, but might more accurately have been called European disunity, agreed that the Federal Republic should join NATO. The three Western powers agreed to end the occupation of their zones of West Germany, though not of West Berlin. The French refused to ratify EDC. This led to an agonising reappraisal not by Dulles but by Eden. One morning he got it: Britain would undertake to keep considerable forces in Europe under NATO for an indefinite period. In announcing this 'very formidable step' he pointed out: 'We are still an island people in thought and tradition, whatever the modern facts of weapons and strategy may compel.' A fair comment, showing how tentative and slow our approach to 'Europe' had been. It was to continue at a similar tempo. On the issue of British forces for Europe Eden and Dulles were at one and he thanked Dulles for his support. Eden considered that the West could now negotiate with the USSR from a base of political and military strength. The USSR possessed that already and was stiffened in its resolve to maintain it by every move that the West made to strengthen the Federal Republic.

A small episode on a big subject illustrates how amateurishly we ran our diplomacy then, as on the whole we still do. Eden called a meeting in his room at the House of Commons to help him draft his winding-up speech in a far-ranging debate. He was in a nervy mood. At one point he demanded to know whether it was possible for an H-bomb test to go undetected. No scientists were present and no one replied, but as I was head of the FO department dealing with the diplomatic and strategic implications of such matters I piped up and said that I thought it was. Almost no one is less scientifically trained than I, but I was right on this point. Eden grunted and when he made his speech got it slightly wrong. The next day the *Daily Express* added to the confusion by headlining its report: 'And now, the silent H bomb.'

In the Middle East, and particularly Iran, Eden was still at loggerheads with the Americans and many others besides. He complained that the US government were neutral in our dispute with Musaddiq instead of wholly backing us. It is the familiar complaint based on a failure to see that American interests are not identical with ours. Britain's interests, as he saw it, were twofold: the government's chief concern was for the sanctity of contracts, while the company had to look after its shareholders. The Security Council adjourned its debate on the British complaint until The Hague court had pronounced on its competence in the oil dispute. Eden stigmatised this as a dismal failure. Writing in 1960 he reflects that breaches of international engagements were not in the middle 1950s as frequent as they have since unhappily become. He should know, for he committed a major breach in 1956. The International Court were not pro-British either: they decided that they had no jurisdiction. When the US government proposed a compromise involving a considerable reduction in the number of British technicians in Iran Eden refused and again lamented the lack of Anglo-American unity. What he does not mention is that Anglo-Iranian relations were eventually restored thanks mainly to the skilful and sustained efforts of the Central Intelligence Agency who brought about Musaddiq's removal. The cost to Britain was the disappearance of our colonial-style position in the oil-fields. The rewards, as anyone can see at Abadan today, were greater production and far friendlier relations with the Iranians, whether officials, businessmen or technicians.

A temporary improvement in Anglo-Egyptian relations was also brought about by the signing of an agreement in October 1954. This provided for the evacuation of our Suez Canal base, to which our legal rights were in any case doubtful. Churchill did not like this withdrawal, but Eden insisted that in the nuclear age the base was yearly less important. This was perhaps an amateurish bit of strategy amounting to a rationalisation. But the important thing was that the previous discord could now be relieved if we had the will to observe this treaty better than we had observed the 1936 one. Both parties undertook to uphold the 1888 Convention guaranteeing freedom of navigation of the Canal, which Eden considered, mistakenly, to be 'of supreme importance' not only to Britain but to the US. Anthony Nutting, the rising young Minister of State at the FO who at that stage worked closely with his friend Eden, signed the agreement.

Eden was pleased with two other diplomatic successes of 1954. One was the shelving of the question to whom did the Buraimi oasis in the middle of Arabia belong. The other was the Trieste settlement which he nostalgically recommended as a rare contemporary example of old-fashioned diplomacy entailing 'open covenants secretly arrived at'.

That then was the tally, and on the face of it it was pretty impressive. Deep down, and in the longer run, it was less so. Certainly the settlement with Iran, which Eden regarded as a

British defeat, has led to continuing good relations and good business. The relatively unimportant Trieste and Buraimi settlements have endured too, though the latter will no doubt be disturbed again one day. But Indo-China, Egypt and Europe were to flare up again, and very dangerously. And the West had allowed one most important opportunity to go by default. In 1954 we received our first firm intelligence on the incipient realisation of something which had so far seemed only wishful thinking on our part: a split between the USSR and China. This was an opportunity that should have been immediately exploited, though of course with care and subtlety rather than the heavy hand. But our energies were too much devoted to lower priority, and less exploitable, matters; and our outlook was too rigid. They were all commies together, and that was that. So such propaganda and divisive techniques as we possessed were not put to good use.

Eden deserves credit for the part he played in bringing about these temporary settlements. But it is not helpful fourteen years later to hark back to a sort of *annus mirabilis* with the suggestion that the methods used then, and the agreements reached, can solve our problems today. It is not impossible that the USSR will one day agree to co-chair a meeting on Vietnam. But if she should it will not be from any blind faith in the 'sanctity' of the old arrangements. It will be because a new juncture has been reached where they provide convenient machinery. In Europe the fearful crises of 1961 and 1962 over the Berlin Wall – I saw it all at first hand as British minister in Berlin – have been surmounted, and our thoughts should no longer be of strengthening NATO but of modifying it with the eventual object of abolishing both it and the Warsaw Pact Organisation. As for Egypt, we shall see how much Eden contributed to causing utter chaos in the Middle East which has led direct to today's explosive situation.

At the end of 1954 Eden and the FO could foresee none of this. What he saw was the light at the end of the long tunnel.

Churchill had been particularly heartless over the succession question in 1953 and 1954. When in bed after another stroke in July 1953 he remarked: 'I don't think I shall ever get well, but I shall not make any decisions until September. Anthony will mew a good deal.' Eden then fell seriously ill himself, but even when he recovered Churchill insisted that he would carry on. In June 1954 Churchill again told Eden that he did not intend to resign at present. 'I don't know if he has accepted it. He'd better.' In July Churchill commented that the Tories had given Eden a poor reception on his return from the Geneva conference, adding rather ungenerously that its results were nothing to be pleased about. He implored him most earnestly once more not to quarrel with the US. In August he declared that he would go in a year's time. In December he had pulled the date back to the following June. But at long last he plumped for April 1955. Young Eden, now nearer sixty than fifty, was finally to succeed; possibly – and why not? – for as long as he had acted the heir apparent. Churchill's own comment was not optimistic: 'I'm sorry for Anthony. He may easily flop, though I shall protect him as far as I can.'

ELEVEN

Number Ten

ON 6TH APRIL 1955 Eden became Prime Minister. He was determined to show that, at last, he was master in his own house. Writing five years later he recorded that he had never felt that he forfeited the nation's confidence. In one sense this was true: he never possessed it in the first place, as Churchill and Attlee had. He was known of course as Churchill's deputy and choice, but above all as the expert on diplomacy; and in Britain in 1955 diplomacy was still considered an esoteric matter which hardly concerned ordinary people and was carried on by specially trained members of the upper classes. So it is in 1968. Bevin's memory was cherished but he was regarded as a sport. Eden chose a great predominance of Old Etonians for his Cabinet, as was to be expected. Mr Butler went to the Treasury, Mr Macmillan to the FO. Only three members out of seventeen had not been to a major public school and Cambridge or Oxford. Four days after Eden took over Churchill remarked, a bit unkindly, that he thought he was already feeling the strain. He confessed in private that he had overpromoted Eden. He had chosen him to succeed at a time when nobody else thought of him as a possible PM. By 1955 some other leading Conservatives who would have welcomed him as leader in 1951 or even 1945 were beginning to have their doubts. Macmillan, waiting in the wings, commented that Churchill had harried Eden so much over the years that he was afraid to make a decision on his own. He also thought him a brilliant negotiator, quiet and persuasive. 'Brilliant' is a dangerous word; and the question now was, in any case, in a different context. Would his qualities, combined with his generally nervy condition, make him a good Prime Minister?

Eden attempted to sort out his broader, including economic, ideas as a preparation for his broader duties. The results were amateurish; and in the end he always came back to diplomacy. He saw it as the first duty of the Western powers to stem the Communist hordes, as he called them. For this purpose he wanted his 'property-owning democracy' – a cliché revived – which he judged was more in the British character than socialism was. In order to impress other nations we needed efficiency in industry, a sense of thrusting well-being and no more nationalisation. Profit was the right motive, and the Americans understood this more wholesomely than many of our people. As many grades of workers as possible should be given a share in the profits. As a result of this lucid and cogent thinking he felt that 'the people' understood and backed him throughout. But the Press, the broadcasters and of course the opposition did not seem to hoist in his national destiny.

Nor was he easy to know personally. More than one of his long-established friends has commented that he knew him no better after twenty years than at the beginning. He was not clubbable and did not care for the smoking-room. To his civil servants he was usually considerate but under pressure he became snappy. Lord Chandos relates that after Eden had rebuked someone in the House one day he said to him: 'I hope I didn't put so-and-so down too hard.' Chandos replied: 'My dear, I thought that your commination was more like a caress.' In fact, though Eden had been in public life all his career and was photographically familiar to people, few could understand just what made him tick.

In the Soviet Union some rather different characters were now installed in power. Malenkov was succeeded by Bulganin in double harness with Khrushchev – the first B & K team. Eden made efforts to establish a rapport with them but the basic differences of character and approach were too great. Churchill in his heyday would surely have hit it off with the rambunctious Khrushchev. In May, West Germany was admitted to NATO and the Soviet government peevishly annulled its treaties with Britain and France, an empty gesture. Nevertheless they also agreed out of the blue to sign with the US, Britain, and France the Vienna treaty giving Austria back her independence. A further proof that B & K were on the move was their visit to breakaway Yugoslavia where they signed a treaty of friendship. In Britain Eden wanted confirmation that he was loved for himself and not merely as Churchill's nominee, and he appeared to get it in the May General Election when the Conservative overall majority rose to a handy sixty.

Eden was now determined to hold the meeting at the summit which had been denied Churchill, though Eisenhower and Dulles were still none too keen. He planned that the meeting should aim at some 'definite if limited' result, but in fact proposed a sweeping agenda: Austria, Germany and European security first; a study of ways of dealing with all other East-West issues after that. Austria was dealt with separately; and on the rest improvement was achieved only under one secondary heading. Eden's tactics in practice were exactly the same as those that had led nowhere in earlier meetings of Foreign Ministers. He placed German reunification in the forefront and insisted that the West must put forward proposals which the Soviet government would find it difficult to reject. Unfortunately no horse of that particular colour existed. The Soviet representatives stood pat. They did not want German reunification at any price. They would not allow it. The situation is the same to this day.

President Eisenhower, briefed by Dulles, started the meeting in Geneva in July 1955 on the wrong foot. He said that the American people held strongly that certain peoples of Eastern Europe had not been given the right to choose their own form of government. Bulganin riposted, in relatively polite terms, that that was none of the President's business.

Now that West Germany was an ally in NATO and was being rearmed the security of Europe precluded any possibility of German reunification. It would have to wait indefinitely. Some sensible discussion took place between the two sides on the possibility of an eventual get-together between NATO and the Warsaw Pact powers and of some agreement about forces and armaments in Germany and neighbouring countries. But when Eden suggested that the Foreign Ministers, who were to take matters further, should place Germany top of the agenda, the Russians insisted that security and disarmament should come before it. So once more there was deadlock. Eden judged that the meeting was worthwhile, however, if only for the discreet improvement it brought about in the Formosa Strait. Out of the summit of the mountain emerged a ridiculous mouse.

Back at home the sound economic base needed for the exercise of effective diplomacy abroad was by no means established. Eden railed at purchase tax, but Butler had to bring in an autumn budget increasing it. Eden wondered whether a reduction in the beer duty might not help as it would, in his own words, 'take (is it two points?) off the cost-of-living index'. He felt that Hugh Gaitskell's election to succeed Attlee as leader of the Labour Party was a national misfortune. They never got on terms and Eden was unable to understand the workings of Gaitskell's mind. This was to prove a fatal factor for Eden over Suez. He consoled himself after a speech at Bradford with the reflexion that, as so often in his life, he had found direct contact with the people a stimulus and a corrective. The delusion here was that he often had any direct contact with 'the people'. If only he had had more the stimulus and corrective might have been more powerful. It is analogous to his delusion that in the sphere of diplomacy he always got on so smoothly with his French and American colleagues – well, almost always. Such delusions are an unsound basis for domestic policy and for diplomacy. That is why the basis cracked and crumbled so suddenly and catastrophically in 1956.

In October the four Foreign Ministers duly met and duly failed to agree on Germany. How could they agree? These four important and busy men – Dulles, Molotov, Macmillan and Pinay – spent nearly three weeks on a futile exercise that moved matters forward not an inch. And in the Middle East the situation was looking ominous. Nasser was working steadily to get all the advantages he could from the US, the USSR and Britain so as to strengthen his independent line. Turkey and Iraq, under Nuri Pasha who was so faithful to his Western allies, signed with our blessing the Bagdad Pact which Eden hoped would grow into a great anti-Soviet coalition in the Middle East. He was mistaken on two counts. First, the Soviet government were spreading their influence in that part of the world by more subtle means than a massive frontal attack – by commercial, technical, military and diplomatic aid and sometimes political infiltration. Secondly, some Middle Eastern peoples were 'on our side' but decidedly the majority preferred to wait and see what they could get out of the Big Power contest. Jordan, so far treated almost as a British colony, was one of these. And finally our actual colony in those parts, Cyprus, was in turmoil. Eden's old Eton friend Henry Hopkinson had left the FO to become a junior minister at the Colonial Office and had used the highly undiplomatic word 'never' when asked about the possibility of Cyprus' independence. Eden himself had rudely brushed aside the suggestion by the Greek Prime Minister, Field-Marshal Papagos, that there was a Cyprus problem to be discussed. But indeed there was, as the mounting terrorism in Cyprus and effervescence on the subject in Greece and Turkey amply proved.

Field-Marshal Harding was recalled from retirement to replace the stock colonial governor and to cope with the emergency in September 1955. He and Lady Harding were brave as lions, and he was so small (she was even tinier) that a jokey friend had suggested that he should ride a Shetland pony at the Queen's coronation instead of the normal-sized horse. Her calmness was exemplified in her reaction to hearing an ominious ticking under her bed one night. She rang for a servant, and asked him to get a bomb-disposal expert to take the nasty thing away, which he did with success. The next morning the servants, who were still Greek Cypriots, were paraded and one was missing. (He turned up some years later and claimed two weeks' wages in lieu of notice. The Governor's ADC spoke to him unprintably.) Belatedly, these servants were replaced by British servicemen. Altogether Harding did not cope very well, and Sir Hugh Foot and the rest of us had to clear up the mess as best we could in 1958 and 1959. (I was by then Political Representative with the Middle East Forces in southern Cyprus, with ambassadorial rank.) The insignificant Buraimi oasis problem also raised its head again. Eden saw King Saud as a pernicious influence: a medieval monarch playing the Soviet game with money paid him by the American oil companies. He therefore encouraged the re-occupation of the oasis by the British-protected Sheikh of Abu Dhabi and Sultan of Muscat. Only during the Suez crisis did he learn that the Americans had told the Australians and the Dutch, without bothering to tell Eden, that they considered this an act of aggression, which he firmly, but by then too late, rebutted.

These were some of Eden's diplomatic difficulties. He and Macmillan added to them unwittingly by denying Marcus Lipton's suggestion in the House that Kim Philby had been the third man in the Burgess-Maclean affair of 1951. At that time Philby was fed up with hanging about and would have liked to go to his 'home', the USSR. These statements gave him a new lease of life and seven more years of active spying against Britain and her friends. Such difficulties combined with difficulties at home, where the Press was highly critical of his administration and Butler's hard budget was not popular, to lead him to take two steps in December 1955. One was normal. He reshuffled his Cabinet, making Butler Lord Privy Seal, the tough and able Macmillan Chancellor, and the colourless Selwyn Lloyd Foreign Secretary. From now on he would be more than ever in charge of foreign affairs. In the 1930s he had been on the receiving end with Chamberlain wielding the power. Now he was the Chamberlain. It was not a hopeful precedent and the outcome was similarly disastrous. The other step was highly unusual for a Prime Minister of only eight months' standing. In reply to criticisms and suggestions he issued a statement that he had no intention of stepping down, that he would continue as before in full control of the situation, and that there was no basis for any innuendoes or hints to the contrary.

By January 1956 the Middle East was in an explosive state. Eden attributed this mainly to Moscow's increasing determination to intrude in Middle East affairs. I was in a position to see British and American intelligence on the situation at the time and I think Eden's analysis is inaccurate and inadequate. Certainly the Soviet Union was expanding its influence in the states which had previously been under British or French domination. There was nothing particularly 'intrusive' about this. The states in question welcomed it and it was mainly done by means of trade, including trade in arms, a means which we had traditionally used ourselves. There was little attempt to impose Communist doctrine. Even today the Communists have not taken over in any Middle Eastern or African state. Nasser and those who sided with him welcomed every opportunity of playing off West against East; and he was all for stirring things up, particularly in connexion with Israel, so as to loosen the grip of Western influence. In February 1955 his guerrillas, the fedayeen, had taken a pounding at the hands of the Israelis. In the same month, on the pro-Western side of the fence, Turkey and Iraq had signed the Bagdad Pact. Britain joined in April, and Eden optimistically judged that the pact, when extended, would bring stability to the area. On the contrary it nettled Nasser into his first arms deal with the Communists, specifically Czechoslovakia, in September 1955. The pact did not meet with US approval either and Eden reflects sadly that we and the US needed to draw together on the prickly topic of colonialism.

Even King Saud and the Greek Cypriots were combining, not of course expressly but negatively, to help the Nasserite cause by their actions against Britain and her client states. One of the chief of these, Jordan, was in a horribly embarrassing position. This small neighbour of Israel had at one and the same time to show Nasser that she was eager to harm Israel, and to preserve her financial and military support from the West. Nasser was hard at work with bribes and assassination plans in Jordan. King Hussein begged to be let off joining the Bagdad Pact because of the further handle it would give to Nasser's propaganda and indeed popularity in Jordan. Our ambassador, Charles Duke, in January 1956 telegraphed that we ought immediately to despatch at least two British brigades to Amman. Nuri Pasha, our chief client in Iraq, wanted American pressure on Nasser to stop his tricks and incidents. It all sounded like a past age. It was. Even so we were not up with the times. Our diplomacy was operating in the last age but one. It could accordingly never be more than temporarily successful. And when the crashes came that were bound to come, first in 1956 and then in 1958, they were all the more catastrophic. We can hear their reverberations today, and so we shall for many a year to come.

In Egypt itself, curiously enough, the US and ourselves were briefly more in accord on our policy. While trying ineffectually to dissuade Nasser from his revolutionary interference in other Arab states, we were engaging in more effectual discussions about massive financial support for the building of the Aswan High Dam. Even so Eden grumbles at the US government's tendency to put inadequate weight behind their friends and preferring to concentrate on becoming more popular with their foes. This is a criticism that has often been made of British diplomacy too. In the present case it arose from Eden's, and the FO's, besetting sin of assuming that the US government's priority list of interests was exactly the same as our own.

In February 1956 Eden visited Eisenhower in Washington, largely to discuss the Middle East. Eden felt that the visit went well enough; work plodded on with no more than the expected difficulties. Later however he reflected that he probably over-valued the political results of his visit, and he was right in this. The communiqué issued at the end had as its real basis an agreement to disagree on Middle Eastern issues as and when considered appropriate by either party. It was as useful as paper can ever be for covering up cracks. It was dangerous because Eden, in the mood that was now settling upon him, chose to interpret it as promising American support for his various policies in the Middle East.

These policies were about to be shaken rigid by the actions of the little man who was generally considered to be our most faithful friend in the Middle East; and by Eden's violent reactions.

TWELVE

The Road to Suez

KING HUSSEIN OF Jordan is a courteous and courageous man. I have enjoyed his company and his country. His Harrovian manners and his good command of English, as well as his liking for fast English cars, have deluded many British diplomats and officers into thinking that he is completely 'one of us.' In fact of course he is the ruler of a non-viable Arab state cut off from the Mediterranean by Israel and reduced to one port on the Red Sea. It is remarkable that he and his country have survived as well as they have. While depending on American and British aid for their survival, since the richer Arab states have never contributed much, the Jordanians have to make big anti-Israel gestures to convince the Arab republics of their basic solidarity and their 'independence' of the West. Add to this a history of mental instability in Hussein's family – his father had to step down from the throne and retire from the world – and the size of Hussein's problems becomes apparent.

On 1st March 1956 Hussein dismissed Glubb Pasha at a moment's notice from his long-established command of the Arab Legion, which he had built up into the most efficient Arab fighting force. This action produced a wide variety of reactions. Selwyn Lloyd, the Foreign Secretary, happened to be in Cairo at the time. Nasser congratulated him on the cleverness of this, he assumed, British-inspired move. Lloyd was not amused. Glubb himself took his removal with dignity and urged Eden to be patient with the young king. Ambassador Duke in Amman recommended that we should not take the matter too tragically. But Eden flew clean off the handle. He considered that Glubb had been treated like 'a pilfering servant'. When he learnt that mobs were cheering Hussein and Nasser in one breath he commented that this was proof that the King had got himself into a false position. This was a mistaken interpretation. In reality Hussein, by getting rid of a British patron of the old school, had won back much of the popularity which Nasser had so dangerously acquired in Jordan, and this at no cost to the country since the Arab Legion continued to function efficiently and Western support also continued after the brouhaha had subsided.

The King told the British ambassador that he was doing the right thing which would prove in the long run to be in the British interest as well. He was right, for it enabled him and Jordan to survive. But Eden sent him an unctuous message about severe blows to confidence on which alone could relations flourish, etc. The tenor of his reply to a message from the Jordanian government calling for cool-ness and prudence made it clear that he had lost his temper, which is rarely a good diplomatic gambit and then strictly only when the losing is deliberate and under control. And in the immediate debate in the House Eden lost his head as well. He made – and he sadly realised it – one of his worst speeches, combining petulant condemnation with a heavy reliance on the familiar but always unconvincing FO gambit that he was not yet in possession of full information. He was roughly handled in the debate. Randolph Churchill wrote scathingly in the *Evening Standard*: 'I was told that the Prime Minister was doing his best. I do not doubt it and that is why I am sure there has got to be, and quickly, a change at 10 Downing Street.' Ian Waller wrote: 'If the year goes on as it has begun it will not be Sir Anthony Eden but Harold Macmillan who reigns in Downing Street in 1957.' He was the first to make publicly this accurate prediction. All this was taking place less than a year after Eden had become Prime Minister. His Cabinet colleagues were worried but remained loyal, though some ambitious thoughts must have crossed Macmillan's mind. The public were puzzled but did not take the whole affair too tragically.

Eden's health deteriorated. His temper grew shorter and he came to depend a good deal on tranquillising and soporific pills. I have it from both a Cabinet minister and a top official that he was on occasions impossible to deal with. But his Cabinet and his diplomats did not stem the progress to doom nor do much to contain the multifarious blunderings. And even Eden's own memoirs, careful as they are to present his side of every question, relentlessly reveal between the lines the grim facts not contained in the printed words.

Thus Eden reflected euphorically on the April visit to Britain of Bulganin and Khrushchev that much good had come of his personal contacts with them. This interpretation is untenable. The first thing to happen on their arrival was that frogman Crabb was found swimming about under their Soviet cruiser, hardly creating an atmosphere of trust and goodwill. On this incident Eden refused to be drawn in the House beyond saying that it had occurred without the knowledge of ministers. This was true but did not encourage confidence in the government's control. The Chief of the Secret Service was sacked, his FO adviser promoted for his pains. Sir Dick White and I, respectively, succeeded them. Eden further pointed out that there was ample precedent for a government refusing to disclose matters on which, in its opinion, publicity could harm the national interest. This too was correct, but here was one of a series of cases where 'the national interest' was to be equated with 'Eden's interest' – a dangerous tendency from which we are not free in our politics today. The Official Secrets Acts are intended to protect the nation as such and not the government of the day. Eden tried again to manipulate them over Suez. In any case the Crabb affair could have been handled more openly with less harm to all concerned. What had happened was that a friend of mine who was Foreign Office Adviser to the Secret Intelligence Service was faced with the Crabb scheme at the end of an exceptionally hard day, during which his father had died. It is understandable that in a distraught moment he approved instead of seeking higher authority, and poor Crabb was first discovered and finally lost as a result. Bulganin and Khrushchev took the incident very well, but they must have wondered a bit. Khrushchev remarked that the *Ordzhonikidze* was an out-of-date vessel that carried no secret equipment and was only suitable for ceremonial purposes. He sold it to Indonesia shortly afterwards.

On the substance of their discussions with him on the Middle East Eden took an aggressive tone. Having in mind that it was traditional Russian policy to try to get through to the warm waters of the Persian Gulf, he told them bluntly to keep their hands off since we would fight for the oil which was our lifeblood. This was an astonishing statement, on several counts. First, we were in no position to fight the USSR in the Persian Gulf or anywhere else. Secondly, it was an exaggeration to call the oil our lifeblood. Thirdly, this was hardly a diplomatic approach to our guests and it gave Khrushchev an opportunity which he did not miss. He piously replied that if Eden was talking about starting a war he could hardly expect sympathy from the Soviet government, who went firmly on the principle that they would only fight in the event of an attack on a member of the Warsaw Pact. Eden, on the usual assumption that Communists never tell the truth, regarded this as mere propaganda; but events have shown that it was a factual statement of policy. Khrushchev went on that if Eden's statement was a threat, the Soviet government rejected it. Eden thereupon repeated his statement, commenting that he was not threatening anybody. He believed that this effectively caused the Soviet government to act 'prudently' over Suez. In fact B and K must have been dumbfounded that Eden, with the limited power at his command, could address the Soviet government in this arrogant fashion. Even if Khrushchev was driven by George Brown's bad manners at dinner to say that he would vote Tory rather than Labour, he can only have gained from his acquaintance with Eden the strongest doubts of his judgment and of his diplomacy. This was, after all, the first ever visit to Britain by the top people in the Soviet government. To say the least they had hardly been treated with due courtesy. And of course the astonishing exchange with Eden over the Middle East had not the slightest moderating effect on Soviet policy over Suez. However, as a result of Suez and its years' long aftermath, the Soviet fleet is now able to show the flag in the Persian Gulf.

To complicate matters in the Middle East the heavy hand was being used over Cyprus with the lack of success that might have been expected. Eden and the Colonial Office, who ruled Cyprus, chose to regard the problem as an administrative one rather than as a highly diplomatic one involving Greece and Turkey. The FO at this stage had little say, for the same narrow reason. Field-Marshal Harding, faced with what was to him a new kind of problem, seemed to find it difficult to cope with the international politics of the matter. Archbishop Makarios, admittedly a maddening man as I discovered later in my personal contacts with him, was deported to the Seychelles. He told me suavely that this nineteenth-century-style measure gave him time to improve his English. We were now up against frank hostility by both Greece and Turkey. In Cyprus itself Major-General Kendrew, a brave man but not a modern-minded commander, deployed thirty thousand troops without first procuring adequate intelligence on where they should winkle out the insurgents. They presented a beautifully broad and vulnerable backside for the terrorists to pepper. Naturally enough we got little sympathy from the US government over these international complications which we chose to handle in the colonial framework. As for the United Nations, Eden found it 'steeped in anti-colonial prejudice' which nevertheless allowed the Soviet 'Moloch' to get away with 'by far the greatest colonial possessions on earth'.

Nasser's forward policy was by now on the march in all directions. Guerrilla attacks on Israel were constant and growing in ferocity. He signed a military alliance with Saudi Arabia and Yemen – strange bedfellows. The departure of the last British troops from the Suez Canal base in June was celebrated as a great victory for him. All these attitudes, and in particular his reiterated assertion that he would smash Israel, became too much for Dulles. On 19th July he curtly told the Egyptian ambassador in Washington that the offer of aid for the Aswan Dam was off. Eden justifiably complained that we were not consulted, but we followed suit the next day. Nasser's riposte came on 26th July when he announced the nationalisation of the Suez Canal. This was in fact doomsday for Eden.

From then on for three months he worked in a sort of frenzy which sometimes touched hysteria. As a result issue after issue was misjudged. On 26th July itself the Cabinet reached the conclusion that the economic life of Europe was threatened with disruption by the Egyptian seizure of the canal. This was a gross exaggeration. Eden wrote in a telegram the next day that a man with Colonel Nasser's record – he was in fact President Nasser, and this is a revealing inaccuracy – could not be allowed 'to have his thumb on our windpipe'. Emotional terms like 'lifeblood' and 'windpipe' came easily to Eden. If the canal were not made international again all our interests in the Middle East would 'inevitably' disappear; we 'could not stop short of using force' to protect our position, even if we had to act alone.

The truth was even more extreme. Eden was determined from the start to use force. Like Hitler and Mussolini, he had to have his war. An inner Cabinet committee of Eden's more amenable colleagues was set up, and this became known as 'the pretext committee'. The Chiefs of Staff were immediately instructed to prepare a plan, including a timetable, for 'an operation designed to occupy and secure the canal'. That is a highly disingenuous way of putting it, as we shall see. Eden records that he expected the US to be 'at least neutral'.

This is where I came in. I was enjoying a marvellous holiday with my family in the Tessin. I had no sooner read on 27th July the news of Nasser's action, which the Swiss newspapers took calmly enough, than I received a telegram from Patrick Dean asking me to return to the FO immediately. Dean was the Assistant Under-Secretary responsible for all relations with the fighting and intelligence services. He was chairman of the Joint Intelligence Committee which contained representatives, at major-general level, of the three services, MI5, MI6, the Joint Intelligence Bureau, and the Commonwealth Relations and Colonial Offices. The CIA representative attended some meetings. It reported to the Chiefs of Staff and to ministers, through the Permanent Under-Secretary, the late Sir Ivone Kirkpatrick. I was Dean's deputy in everything, including chairing the Deputy Directors' JIC, as head of the Permanent Under-Secretary's department with the rank of Counsellor. I was also the only civilian to sit regularly with the Joint Planning Staff which otherwise comprised representatives of the three services. Kirkpatrick, Dean or I often attended meetings of the Chiefs of Staff. So I had a good purview.

Our instructions, passed down by word of mouth from Eden, were both clear and unusual. First, only we three were to be in on all the intelligence and planning. (The three were to be reduced to two at a later stage.) Other under-secretaries, for instance the experts on economic matters, Middle Eastern problems, or Anglo-American relations, were to be kept in the dark as far as possible. The task was to be given top priority as well as top secrecy. And the object of our plan was to be to topple Nasser, by force of course as this could not be done otherwise. This was Eden's last vendetta, and it was to end like the others but with more disastrous results for the country. The pretence, for public purposes, had to be that we were preparing a limited contingency plan which it was hoped would never have to be used. The truth was otherwise. We were under orders to get ready a plan for the invasion of Egypt at the earliest possible date. General

133

Stockwell, the Commander of the Land Forces, has quoted his own directive: 'To prepare to mount a joint operation against Egypt to restore the Suez Canal to international control.' That was sweeping and open enough; in fact it went as near to saying 'Topple Nasser by any means' as a rather widely circulated directive in black and white could prudently do. Of course political suggestions from various countries and quarters would have to be given apparent consideration as they came up. Then Eden could say, in that strikingly original way of his, that no avenue had been left unexplored nor stone unturned. But Eden's eye was fanatically fixed on the removal of 'the dictator'. As a result evasion and deviousness were the watchwords throughout August, September and October. As a further result our military and political plans, based as they were on so many illusions and misjudgments, ended in disaster.

Eden's miscalculation of the US government's attitude and policy was apparent from the start, though again this was not made clear to the public or even to the FO at the time. He telegraphed to President Eisenhower on 27th July: 'If we do not take a firm line our influence and yours throughout the Middle East will be finally destroyed.' Here he was mistakenly equating the American position with our own and giving unsolicited advice into the bargain. 'We should not allow ourselves to become involved in legal quibbles about the rights of the Egyptian government to nationalise what is technically an Egyptian company.' The FO legal adviser's firmly, but vainly, expressed view that these were no 'quibbles' and that the company was indeed Egyptian, not just technically, was brushed aside. 'The first step must be for you and us and France to align our policies.' Eden conceded that our reply to Nasser must take account of what he called 'the modern trend towards internationalism and away from nationalism'. In practice however, he went blindly down what he saw as the British national road and never seriously brought the United Nations into the matter. Consequently it was Eden and Britain who were eventually arraigned by the United Nations and forced to abandon their aggression.

Eden was given fair warning early on from two important quarters that he would get no support for the use of naked force. Our ambassador in Washington, Sir Roger Makins, reported on 30th July that the State Department were cool and hesitant about any question of urgent action, and the President made it clear that he would not go along with it. Eden reports that Eisenhower did not rule out the eventual use of force; but this sounds, to put it politely, like wishful recollecting and does not tally with Eisenhower's own statements. And on 2nd August Hugh Gaitskell warned that the Opposition would resist any use of force not approved by the United Nations. This raised Eden's hackles for various reasons. He disliked Gaitskell personally. He considered that he and the Labour Party did not understand military matters and were more or less a bunch of pacifists. He hated the United Nations because they did not always support British policy. Finally, he was already in the mood to see his war as a national crusade which it was the Opposition's duty to support. This was to lead him later to attempt some distinctly dictatorial measures. Meanwhile in his speeches, as in those of others on both sides of the House, Nasser was compared with Hitler – did he not encourage his officers to read *Mein Kampf*? – and Mussolini. This comparison was intended to drum up the martial zeal of the British people, and fell pretty flat. Eden expressed amazement at the fact that 'left-wing national leaders' seemed to admire Nasser more than the elderly and paternalistic figure of Nuri Pasha, our client in Iraq. And, crisis or no crisis, parliament duly broke up for the summer holidays on 2nd August.

Eden now went to work in the style of the 1930s. The Constantinople Convention of 1888 had guaranteed the use of the Canal 'for all the world and for all time'. But what was the use of quoting such outdated generalisations? They were bound to madden Nasser without affecting his policy, and they could not be made to work in the conditions of the

1950s. Nasser was said to threaten the freedom and security of the canal. It may have looked like that to many people in the heat of the moment, but it was not correct. Finally, respect would be shown for legitimate Egyptian interests. Nasser's reaction to that was: thank you for nothing, it certainly will, and we will see to it, not you. As for the United Nations, no initiative by the 'free nations' could succeed because it would be opposed by the Afro-Asian 'extremists' – Eden's word for 'representatives' – supported by the USSR. Doubts about British national unity behind Eden, which were well justified, helped to weaken American resolution. Our ambassador in Washington reported that the problems raised by any question of using force in an election year would be appalling. Eden paid no attention. 'Following my usual custom I maintained my hopes of American support.'

It was against this background that we officials and officers slogged on with our planning. At an early stage I remember a merry brigadier saying, with modest pride, that he reckoned we could get the troops ashore within three or four months of D-day. I told him we should be lucky on the political side if we had three or four days. Our first plan, called Hamilcar, was based on a landing at Alexandria. This is clear proof that our real instructions were to topple Nasser by taking Cairo, for no one in his senses would land at Alexandria for the purpose of taking over the canal. However we were told to change it and Musketeer was born. This was partly because Eden was by now as obsessed with the canal as he was with Nasser, and partly because it was considered more respectable to go first for the ostensible cause of all the trouble. At first Eden wanted to attack in August. We reported that the state of preparedness of the British forces made this impossible. For one thing the deep-water port in Cyprus on which rapid action would hinge unfortunately did not exist. The French, who were as eager as Eden to topple Nasser because of his subversive activities in Algeria, were prepared to take chances with a parachute drop; but the British military were more cautious. On and on we went, day and night, for weeks and months. New directives would arrive from on high; Musketeer was revised – 'Musketeer A' – re-revised as 'B' and eventually used as a hotch-potch of the lot. My military colleagues enjoyed every minute of it. I myself saw no reason not to do what I was told. In the world of intelligence and planning you get many strange assignments and contingencies.

At the end of August Pat Dean was sensationally promoted over many heads from Assistant Under-Secretary (Grade 4) to Deputy (Grade 2). He was now, unprecedentedly for the job he held, number two in the whole Office and directly below Kirkpatrick. His successors have never been so fortunate. This meant that he not only outranked all the political and economic under-secretaries but all his fellow-members of the JIC too. A good few noses were put out of joint. While we continued in the JIC to collaborate with our US friends we had to take great care that no whiff of our planning activities reached them. Although we had all the hard intelligence at our disposal we did not know all that was going on behind the scenes at the highest level. Or rather, only two of us knew. We planned for a combined Anglo-French operation; and we took it on trust that the most important diplomatic preparations, such as ensuring a favourable attitude on the part of the US government, were being adequately handled by Eden and Selwyn Lloyd.

But this was far from being the case. Dulles did not consider the canal question important enough to come to Britain straight away, and sent the highly able Robert Murphy, Assistant Secretary of State, instead. Eden made to him on 31st July what was surely one of the most outrageous remarks of all his diplomatic career. He would not ask the US government for anything 'but we do hope you will take care of the Bear'. In other words, if the Russians took action the Americans were to fight them, and should this escalate into nuclear warfare, well, it would be in a good cause. Murphy was at pains to explain to Eden that the American interests involved were not identical with the

British. But he noted that Eden never succeeded in adjusting his thoughts to Britain's altered world status, which of course was an objective factor in the whole situation for both the US and Soviet governments. Macmillan, on the other hand, always reckoned with this. Consequently, where Dulles' discussions with Eden were uncomfortable to say the least no such difficulties arose when he was talking with Macmillan. Eden committed the gross error of thinking he could go to Eisenhower over Dulles' head. This was out of the question in practice, and every time he tried it Dulles was naturally annoyed. Murphy records that many Americans found Eden uncongenial and even slippery. Dulles had especially disliked his attitude at the 1954 conference on Indo-China. Hoover frankly 'couldn't stand him'. The President made it clear more than once that he disapproved of what he called 'eighteenth-century tactics' and he insisted on diplomacy instead.

However, while military action was prepared the right thing for Eden was to appear ready to try diplomacy. On the home front Gaitskell asked him on 11th August for an assurance that he would not use force without United Nations approval. This Eden refused to give, and the gap between government and opposition widened from then on. Dulles thought up a meeting of twenty-four nations to discuss the matter. Eden agreed; but predictably Nasser did not. However, the meeting assembled without him and Eden gave a brief opening address. He warned that all had a common interest in the sanctity of agreements. This was not accurate, and the example which he cited of Portuguese Goa was hardly likely to encourage another member, India, to agree. In the end eighteen nations subscribed to a declaration issued on 21st August, with Spain making a minor reservation. All but three of these were strongly capitalist nations. A rival declaration inspired by Pandit Nehru and supported by the USSR, Indonesia and Ceylon called for a purely advisory international board with no control functions. Prime Minister Menzies of Australia took the majority proposals to Nasser for discussion. Eden pretended then and later that there was a good chance that Nasser would accept them. But he must have known, as a great many other people knew, that there was actually not a hope in hell. Nasser had seized the canal and was not going to give it up. The document handed him by Menzies wrapped up in polite verbiage the proposal that he should do just that. This was not diplomacy, but time-wasting. Menzies did not improve his chances by telling Nasser that the London conference had not ruled out the use of force. But at the same moment Dulles was telling the Press that the canal was not of primary importance to the US, a true statement and one which had been clearly made before. Nasser rejected the proposals on 10th September. Menzies reported in words which were sweet to Eden's ear. Egypt was not only a dictatorship but a police state. Nasser was in some ways quite a likable fellow but with irritating mannerisms. He possessed considerable intelligence but was immature. A kind of logical mess existed in his mind. The condescending arrogance of the have nations towards the have-nots has seldom been more pithily expressed.

From now on Eden and Dulles were increasingly at cross-purposes. Eden thought Dulles favoured economic measures, such as the withholding of dues, and complained that nevertheless he would not adopt them. In fact Dulles side-stepped the question. Didactically Eden said that the US government should align their policies strictly with their allies and forget about colonialism. But his tone became steadily more colonialist. M Spaak, the Belgian Foreign Minister, heartened him by saying that he feared the mistakes of the Hitler period might now be repeated. 'So did I,' was Eden's comment. But Dulles, and most other thinking people, saw no parallel. He declared, however, on 30th August that the US government would support an Anglo-French appeal to the Security Council but strictly on the condition that it was an honest attempt to reach a solution and not 'a device for obtaining cover'. This showed that

Dulles was not to be fooled. When the resolution was drafted it began in a way calculated to put up the maximum number of backs: 'Recognising that the arbitrary and unilateral action of the Government of Egypt has disturbed the *status quo.* . . .' On 4th September Dulles made another clear and critical statement to our ambassador. He said that he regarded our position as a weak one judicially. We were threatening force if Egypt refused to accept a new treaty; yet the 1888 Convention gave us all the rights we required. Then a bright, if less lucid, idea: why not form a Suez Canal Users' Association? Eden agreed to go ahead with this and the Security Council resolution together. After all, the military attack was not yet quite ready.

At this stage Eden had an exchange of messages with the President that got him nowhere. He had convinced himself that Dulles had said that Nasser 'must be made to disgorge'. Murphy discounts this. In any case on 3rd September Eisenhower informed Eden that American opinion flatly rejected force. He of course had one eye on the elections, only a couple of months away. Eden replied on 6th September most emotionally. One passage referred to Hitler and the 1930s; another to Russia trying the same tactics. 'Similarly this is an opening gambit in a campaign by Nasser to expel all Western influence from Arab countries. . . . New governments will be Egyptian satellites if not Russian ones. . . . We here shall all be at his mercy. . . . We have many times led Europe in the fight for freedom. It would be an ignoble end to our long history if we accepted to perish by degrees.' And so on. You can picture the President's reaction: say, Foster, is this fella Eden off his rocker?

The Anglo-French resolution was now ready for the Security Council. It ran into two sorts of difficulty before it got there. The FO legal adviser, Sir Gerald Fitzmaurice, pointed out that its legal basis was not impregnable. The US government were more explicit and actually questioned its basis in law. They not only declined to join in sponsoring it; they would not even support it. Dulles accused the sponsors of trying to force a new treaty on Egypt. If the basis was the declaration by the eighteen powers, including the US, Nasser had after all rejected this. Eden could not grasp this point. Dulles urged that the Security Council should simply be informed of the problem and not asked for any action. This was accordingly done. Even so, the USSR used its veto on 14th October.

Meanwhile Dulles had produced his plan for SCUA. The French thought it pretty useless, which it was. Eden however thought it necessary 'to lean over backwards' to work with the US and persuaded the French to accept it. He was a bit late in his leaning; but again it gave time for military preparations, such as the massing of British and French forces in Cyprus, to go forward. The SCUA was set up at a meeting in London on 21st September. It was stillborn. However, in different ways it served both Eden's and Dulles' purposes. When Eden complained that the American attitude to it removed any teeth it might have Dulles riposted: teeth, what teeth? 'There were no teeth in it, so far as I am aware.' Eden came to the bitter conclusion that the American idea was that the SCUA should collect dues for Nasser. Nasser himself had a different description of it: it was 'an association for waging war' and the eighteen powers were guilty of 'international thuggery and imperialism'.

The US government continued to pursue a consistent line. On 11th September the President repeated to the Press what he had already told Eden: he would not back France and Britain should they resort to force. On 13th September Dulles made it plain that the US government would never use force to send American ships through the Canal, though Eden urged that they had every right to do so. Eden reflected in melancholy fashion that close co-operation with the US had been a guiding principle throughout his political life. This is a most doubtful statement; even if true, practice had seldom matched up to principle. Now American cynicism was leading to a 'master and vassal relationship'. The American attitude left no alternative but to use force or to acquiesce in Nasser's 'triumph'. He received solace from a speech on 12th September by Sir Robert Boothby, though he has never been famous for the keenness of his judgment on foreign affairs. This once more harked back to the 1930s and intimated that we should act more forcefully this time. It referred in passing to 'a horrible little book called *A Philosophy of Revolution* which is like a potted version of *Mein Kampf*'. This was of course President Nasser's own book. I wonder whether Sir Robert had in fact studied either of them? At the same time Eden received far less solace from the declaration of a former Conservative Attorney-General, Sir Lionel Heald, that force could not be used unless the United Nations approved. Eden declined to endorse this view. He also antagonised the Indian government who consistently urged a negotiated settlement. He indicated that he would indeed 'negotiate' but only on his own terms; and that Nehru did not share his own view of the importance of keeping international agreements. Dulles harried him by pointing out, truthfully, more than once that public opinion in Britain was not solid behind his policies over Suez. Eden would hear none of this. The national crusade was on, and that was that.

Towards the end of September Macmillan, Chancellor of the Exchequer, was able to report after a visit to Washington that the American attitude was reassuring in many ways. This is curious. Partly it may be that Eden's blind optimism on this point enabled him to interpret Macmillan's views in this way. Partly no doubt Macmillan had got on so much better than Eden with the members of the US administration that relations seemed a bit rosier. But Macmillan's role throughout the crisis needs some explaining. He breathed fire and slaughter with the best. He got his sums all wrong. His final report on the weakness of sterling was one of the decisive factors in causing the collapse of the expedition. And he was right on the spot when it came to the succession. Being the shrewdest of politicians he must have seen early on that Eden's nerve was cracking.

Eden was by now deeply irritated with the United

Nations. Plans for negotiation were bandied about, but as they involved both give and take he condemned them as lacking respect for the sanctity (again) of agreements. He meant, of course, strictly those agreements which appealed to him; for he was on the point of breaking various agreements himself. He again reflected wistfully how good the League of Nations had been in this respect; but he did not reflect on how abject a failure it had proved. He complained that young states did not see that the rule of law was important for them as well as for the haves; and that two standards of conduct were being evolved. There was truth in these statements, for what the young states often do not regard as adequate is the type of law and the type of standards which the rich nations attempt to impose on them. In all this Eden could not understand that if diplomacy is to have any effect it must be as dynamic as the changing world. It may serve to slow down or soften some dangerously harsh developments. But it is misconceived to imagine that it can, or should, preserve some arbitrary *status quo*.

There was a further danger at the United Nations. The Egyptian Foreign Minister, Fawzi, showed signs of being reasonable. Another irritating fact was that the Egyptians were now running the canal as efficiently as it had ever been run, which Eden and many others had declared to be impossible. In Paris Eden and Lloyd agreed with the French that unless the Security Council approved their joint resolution they would use force. In the event the Soviet representative obliged on 14th October by vetoing the resolution.

The first half of October was decisive. On 1st October the SCUA had its futile inaugural meeting. Everyone seemed to whittle away the Anglo-French proposals. On the same day Eden telegraphed to Eisenhower in an attempt to make his blood run cold: 'The wider dangers of the Middle East situation can be summed up in one word: Russia. Nasser is now effectively in Russian hands, just as Mussolini was in Hitler's.' But though Eisenhower, and particularly Dulles, were often prone to alarmism where Communism was concerned they could not swallow this crude analysis whole. Indeed the very next day Dulles spoke pejoratively about 'the colonial powers', and even Eden realised that many Americans agreed with him. In the same statement Dulles kicked the SCUA in the teeth, or rather the gums. When it came to the Soviet veto the US government showed no concern at the Anglo-French defeat. Other powers showed relief. Not a word of censure aimed at Egypt was spoken. 'Plunder had paid off.' Eden reflected that it was 'inevitable' that there would be a reckoning for this 'moral backsliding'.

If the word 'moral' is applicable at all to diplomacy – and we should always remember that there are various systems of morality apart from, and just as highly respected as, the Christian – Eden at exactly this point was in no position to discuss political morality. Deception has undeniably a part to play in diplomacy. In connexion with gathering the intelligence on which to base a sound policy it is often essential, just as it is in war. But certain rules apply. It must be used selectively or it can become a bad habit. It is preferable not to use it against your close colleagues and friends. And most dangerous of all, the diplomat must not get into the situation of deceiving himself.

Inside the FO the atmosphere had become frustrating and tense. People felt that some funny business was going on; only two officials knew what it was. These were Kirkpatrick and Dean. I myself had been in on all the planning and re-planning. I had seen all the intelligence, which indicated that matters were coming to a head between Israel and the Arabs, and in particular Egypt. We also knew that the French were supplying Israel with large quantities of arms and were in very close relations with them. In the FO the pro-Arab faction was traditionally strong. People sympathised with Israel's sufferings at the hands of the guerrillas, but there was little real feeling for a country which had been rough with the British and which now appeared as a brash disturbing element in the Middle East. These feelings about Israel tallied too with Eden's. The Middle Eastern and other

144

experts were kept busy cooking up draft schemes for the Security Council, SCUA and so on; but some of them had an uneasy feeling that Eden's heart was not in that part of the game. And at this period I found that Pat Dean would occasionally disappear in a mysterious manner for twenty-four hours or so. We had connecting offices and frequently popped in on each other with urgent papers or questions. On these occasions I would pop in and find no Dean. Not only so, but his private secretary could not say where he was; and he was far too conscientious a man to have slipped out for a quick one. On his return he vouchsafed no explanation; and, good subordinate official as I then was, I did not press for one.

By the end of September the French were getting impatient. Eden was in the habit of treating them *de haut en bas*. They took it all and were most loyal allies. But into the bargain they had worked out a joint plan with the Israelis under which the latter would attack Egypt and the French would give them military support. Who knows whether this strategy might not have succeeded? But the French decided that they needed British bombers and the air bases in Cyprus to cover the operation. They also decided that the time had come to get Eden in on the collusion act. M Pineau, the French Foreign Minister, broached the matter briefly with Eden on 3rd October on the lines that Israel had now made up her mind to attack within three weeks and what should the Western allies do about it? Eden replied with some inconclusive remark about 'the Jews', though Pineau interpreted it as meaning that he was ready to collaborate. So from now on it was collusion and deception all the way. For a start Israel made threatening noises in the direction of Jordan; and Eden helped by warning Israel ostentatiously that we should help Jordan if attacked. Our ambassador in Amman was not, of course, told of the inwardness of this by Eden or Lloyd. Nor was his most able colleague in Cairo, Sir Humphrey Trevelyan, kept informed of Eden's thoughts and intentions.

In fact only one person was kept fully informed, and that was Selwyn Lloyd. Eden would give the cabinet a rousing but misleading report from time to time. He used Anthony Nutting, then Minister of State at the FO and a Middle East expert, only sporadically, in the intervals of telling him that he did not understand politics. The various other FO ministers such as the Parliamentary Under-Secretary Douglas Dodds-Parker, who was also a Middle East expert, were left wholly in the dark. Patrick Dean was employed as a sort of high-grade messenger or office boy. Kirkpatrick appeared to participate in the enterprise with zest. We more junior officials and officers at least were not instructed to make yet another plan since we were not trusted with the information about collusion. Obviously the plan we had produced should have been radically altered to meet the new situation. In the event it was again tinkered with and proved none too bad in practice.

Another group of people whom Eden and Lloyd have never seen fit to take into their confidence either then or since is the British public as a whole, including the House of Commons. Eden's memoirs are completely silent on the whole matter. Lloyd too has remained entirely mum. This entailed both of them telling lies to the House. Lloyd was rewarded by being made its leader under Macmillan, and Eden with the Earldom of Avon. Much of the truth was related in a book published in France as early as 1957. Nevertheless when Lord Avon was asked by the editor of a leading British Sunday paper whether he would care to write a critique of Professor Hugh Thomas's excellent book on Suez published in 1967[1] he flew into a rage, dismissed it as a pack of lies, and indicated that he would horsewhip Thomas, if he had a horse.

Eden received support for his plans, predictably, from the Conservative annual conference that met in the second week of October 1956. The words 'wogs' and 'wog-bashing', long beloved by sound Tories and particularly those of a military bent, were much heard in the corridors when President

[1] *The Suez Affair*, Hugh Thomas, Weidenfeld and Nicolson, 1967.

Nasser and his fellow-Egyptians were being discussed. The egregious Rab Butler, always so happy to serve as number two or three to anyone, came right out with the statement that he had served under five Prime Ministers and he could assure the assembled faithful that there was none who could vie with Eden in 'flair, courage and integrity'. So much for Winston Churchill, amongst others.

Eden records that when he and Lloyd flew to Paris on 16th October to see M Mollet, the Prime Minister, and M Pineau, there was no lack of material for discussion. This was true indeed. What he does not record is that the die had been cast two days before. On Sunday October 14th M Gazier, the French acting Foreign Minister in M Pineau's temporary absence, and the Deputy Chief of Staff of the French Air Forces, General Challe, had been received by Eden at Chequers. Anthony Nutting was present in place of Selwyn Lloyd who was at the United Nations, witnessing the Anglo-French resolution being vetoed by the USSR. The French delegates proposed to Eden the plan of action, in collusion with Israel, which was put into effect a couple of weeks later. Eden was 'diplomatically' non-committal but as soon as the Frenchmen had left he made it clear to Nutting that this was it. Nutting did not like the plan one bit. He had operated frequently and well at the United Nations and he knew that it would stink in their nostrils. But Eden's mind was made up. He telephoned Lloyd in New York and hailed him back immediately. When he arrived next day Nutting tried to make him see sense. But Lloyd proved, as ever, Eden's faithful henchman.

Eden's account of the discussions in Paris with the French ministers is totally unreliable. It is regrettable that one who had only recently been Prime Minister of Britain (he wrote in 1960) should provide historians of this critical period with such an incomplete record. He does go as far as to say that while Israel must not attack Jordan, it would be another matter if she broke out against Egypt. 'We discussed these matters in all their political and military aspects' – this deliberately vague phrase is the nearest he ever got to admitting the facts of collusion. He still pretended that Her Majesty's Government must wait for Nasser's latest proposals for a settlement and pay due heed to them. He reflected that he had seen it all before, quoting rather obscurely Sarajevo, the usual 1930s, Trieste the year before. On his return to London he saw a number of Cabinet colleagues, taking the precaution to interview them individually. No one has recorded just what he said. His own report is that there was no friction, though there were some differing shades of opinion. He had never known a government more united on an issue of the first importance. But in the first place he did not tell his colleagues the whole truth. And secondly we know from one of them, Anthony Nutting, that this comment is not true either.

The matter was clinched, in a typically hole-and-corner fashion, at tripartite meetings at Sèvres on 22nd and 23rd October. Although the Israeli Prime Minister Ben Gurion, and his French opposite number, Guy Mollet, attended, Eden would not go. He sent instead Lloyd and Dean. Lloyd stayed as short a time as possible and tried to fob off the two Prime Ministers with Dean's signature below theirs on the document of agreement. This annoyed Ben Gurion very much and he insisted that it should be flown to London to obtain a more authoritative signature. Final approval was not given by the Cabinet until 25th October; Eden regarded it as a pure formality. He also tried to force the BBC to broadcast only his news on the forthcoming war because it was all, in his opinion, a united patriotic effort to which there could be no loyal opposition. His old friend Cadogan, at the top of the BBC, would probably have wetly agreed, but there were stouter hearts lower down and this bit of attempted dictatorship was foiled. He also tried to muzzle the Press by means of a 'D notice' prohibiting mention by word or photograph of the movement of troops. When he met leading editors and proprietors they told him straight that the nation was not at war and that it would be idle to expect the British Press not to publish what foreign newspapers were publishing freely. So that attempt failed too. William Clark, whom Eden had brought from *The Observer* to be his PRO at Number Ten, was so disgusted with these manœuvres that he resigned.

Eden's own account of these days is disingenuous, to say the least. Of course he makes no reference whatever to the Sèvres meeting or its product. He remarks that reports on Israeli intentions were conflicting: in fact their intentions were quite clear. Israel mobilised on 27th October and attacked on 29th October. Alfred Robens, shadow Foreign Secretary, was dining with Eden and Lloyd that evening and was told of the invasion. Eden told him how important it was that the opposition should back the government, but when Robens said that obviously we must now consult the French and US governments in accordance with the Tripartite Declaration of 1950 Eden neither agreed nor disagreed. 'When he made his statement in the House of Commons,' reports Robens, 'I was perhaps more surprised than any man in England.' The statement was to the effect that 'we could not stand aside and watch'. The House was asked to believe that, purely in order to prevent the war from spreading, we and the French had selflessly to intervene. By a coincidence we had the necessary military plans all ready, in the shape of those worked out to deal with Nasser's seizure of the canal. Eden remains convinced today 'that we chose the lesser evil'. The Labour opposition immediately asked about collusion but received only a frigid non-reply.

Eden had been at great pains to keep his intentions secret from our closest ally, the Americans. Our ambassador in Washington, Sir Roger Makins, had been withdrawn on 11th October and was not replaced by Sir Harold Caccia until 8th November, when he reached the US by slow boat. The US ambassador in London, Winthrop Aldrich, was systematically fobbed off with flannel, which very much annoyed Eisenhower. When the Israeli invasion began the Americans knew nothing of British or French complicity.

Eden even sent Eisenhower a telegram on the morning of 30th October in which he did not mention the ultimatum which he was to announce the same afternoon. The terms of that notorious ultimatum reached the apex of hypocrisy and absurdity. It called on Egypt and Israel to withdraw ten miles from each side of the canal. The Israeli forces had not got to within ten miles, though Eden suggested otherwise, so they would be at liberty to do a forward withdrawal. The Egyptians would have to withdraw something like a hundred miles. The US government had already urged the Security Council to brand Israel as an aggressor. But at this late stage Eden still thought he could sell the Anglo-French plan to the President. He explained in his second telegram that he would have liked to ask the President to associate himself and his country with the ultimatum, which he thought both sides might well accept. 'It would help very much if you found it possible to support what we have done.' Only Anglo-US collaboration could deal with the Middle East: so much for the faithful French. 'This seems an opportunity for a new start.' I hear an echo of Neville Chamberlain's remark on an earlier issue: this is the very midsummer of madness. Nor had Eden or Lord Home, the Commonwealth Secretary, thought it necessary to inform any Commonwealth country of the government's intentions, for all their talk about the basic importance of Commonwealth solidarity. They were all expected to tag along. Even faithful Australia found this too much to swallow and voted against Britain on one Soviet resolution.

'The US government's reactions,' says Eden, 'were unfavourable.' That was putting it mildly. What is astonishing is that Eden was astonished, and bitter. Mr Cabot Lodge pressed his resolution condemning Eden's 'constructive suggestions' to a vote in the Security Council. For the first time ever on a major issue the US and the USSR were at one. For the first time ever we used our veto. It fell to Sir Pierson Dixon, the gentlest and most intelligent of men, to do so and to explain that our intervention was purely temporary and had no anti-Egyptian character. He did his duty with less than no pleasure. Other important British ambassadors round the world were briefed, but not Sir Humphrey Trevelyan in Cairo; he learnt of developments from the ticker tape. He had no inkling of our bombing campaign until he heard the droning of bombers and found, on looking up at the sky, that they belonged to the RAF. Sir William Hayter heard the news after dinner at the Kremlin: he thought he must be tight. He wrote several letters of resignation but tore them all up. Some other top officials huffed and puffed about resigning; in fact only three juniors did so. The general reaction in the FO was that we did not know whether to laugh or cry at the idiotic stratagem of the ultimatum. A number of under-secretaries signed a round-robin aimed at Kirkpatrick and Lloyd complaining at the way they had been side-tracked. Some were indignant at being left out of the fun. Others sincerely resented being treated with distrust over the months and thus forced to work in a sort of vacuum.

By now the entire Anglo-French politico-military operation was at sixes and sevens, even before the military part of it had got off to its sluggish start. In the House there were immediate questions by the opposition about collusion. Eden fended them off with statements that, in everyday parlance, can only be called lies. In order to comply with the terms of the ridiculous ultimatum which he himself had dreamed up the RAF were not let loose on Egyptian air-fields until dusk on 31st October. He reminisces that the bombing phase, originally planned to take up to a fortnight, was reduced to six days. If it was indeed planned to take a fortnight I have no recollection of it and it must have been a late amendment, perhaps by Eden himself? He certainly tinkered with the military plans up to the last possible moment. Moreover, the British and French fleets steaming doggedly in from Malta and Algeria had jumped the ultimatum gun anyway – a good thing tactically but hardly in keeping with the high moral tone adopted over the whole affair. If they had started out several days before, and the paratroops had been used more daringly, that might have made more sense. For after five days' fighting, as Eden reports, the Israelis had achieved all their main objectives, while their allies were still nowhere.

Now the chickens were coming heavily home to roost from all directions. On the personal side Nutting, whom many in the FO considered the natural successor of Eden in style and ability, confirmed on 31st October the threat he had made on grounds of conscience to resign from the government. Eden, who had helped him in his career and been friendly in his more patient moments, greeted this with a French tag. '*Tout casse sauf l'amitié*,' he said, and has never spoken a word to Nutting since. In the Cabinet Eden tried icily to still some criticism by young Macleod when he said that of course some Cabinet ministers had had no experience of what was needed to govern in wartime. Macleod, who can be icy too, replied that the Cabinet and country had not so far been told that we were at war. In Cyprus the British staff of the propaganda broadcasting station beamed on Cairo downed tools and refused to obey their orders. On 1st November the Opposition moved a vote of censure and there was unprecedented rowdiness, which Eden tiredly deplored. He replied by blackguarding first the United States and then the United Nations. Our own legal system and 'the rule of law' were more important, he stated; while the British bombers continued their operations against Egypt. The government's built-in majority of sixty-nine convinced him that the world agreed with him. At the United Nations however the emphasis was different. Foster Dulles, now very sick with cancer and due for an operation in the near future, took the lead in condemning the tripartite aggression against Egypt. The USSR supported him. His resolution supporting an immediate cease-fire was adopted by 64–5. In spite of this condemnation by the world, and of the practical point of some importance that the Israeli-Egyptian battle was by now almost over, the Anglo-French effort

152

continued. The rest of the grotesque campaign can be briefly summarised. At 8 am on the 5th of November – please to remember – British and French parachutists started to drop. Battered though the Egyptians were, they put up some resistance. On the same day Aneurin Bevan asked whether the government proposed to stop lying to the House of Commons. Eden and Lloyd denied throughout all discussions in the House that any collusion had taken place and have remained silent on the topic ever since. Professor Thomas uses the word 'lie' to describe three of their formal statements; while Nutting generously nails only one as a 'lie' but leans heavily on 'disingenuous' to describe others. In a sense it was a preview of the Profumo case. Meanwhile, the Royal Marine and French commandos went ashore early on 6th November. By 5 pm our forces had reached El Cap, twenty-three miles down the Canal. Ismailia was thirty miles further on. General Keightley, the Allied Commander-in-Chief, told Eden he thought he could occupy Ismailia in another forty-eight hours and Suez by 12th November. With all respect to the General, if he had gone flat out and accepted the proffered Israeli help he could surely have got to both Suez and Cairo in those same forty-eight hours. Certainly the French commanders were game. General Massu, the paratroop leader, later remarked that if he had known what his superior officers intended 'I would have marched to Cairo'. Selwyn Lloyd himself expressed the opinion to a group of journalists that the Anglo-French forces could have finished the job in forty-eight hours. In December Antony Head, Minister of Defence since 18th October, when Sir Walter Monckton gave up on grounds of conscience, altered the story: it would have taken 'about seven days' to get to Suez! However, what actually happened was that at 5 pm on 6th November Keightley received the staggering instruction to cease fire at midnight. The shambles was complete.

It will be a long time before political and military analysts finish commenting on this imbroglio but three authoritative sources are worth quoting here. Foster Dulles, who had done most of all to prevent and then hamstring the adventure, said to Selwyn Lloyd when he visited him in hospital after his cancer operation a few days later: 'Why on earth did you stop?' President Nasser said that he had made two appreciations of the situation in early October, one from his own point of view and one from Eden's. He had concluded that Eden could not be so silly as to use force. Field-Marshal Montgomery, who always speaks his mind, has since commented that he could never for the life of him understand why we went to war over Suez; he was baffled by the whole affair. In brief, Eden had gone to war unnecessarily and in defiance of international law; and into the bargain had botched it.

It is difficult, but worth trying, to weigh the various factors that led to the fiasco. Undoubtedly first was the collapse of Eden's morale and nerve. Probably second was the completeness and outspokenness of American opposition. Then there was the opposition at home which manifested itself in unprecedentedly violent scenes in the House and a monster demonstration on 4th November in Trafalgar Square, followed by a march on Downing Street. Macmillan at last made it clear to Eden that the run on the pound could not be withstood much longer. The US government both backed that run and offered a financial inducement in return for an immediate cease-fire. Nevertheless I think we could have carried on for the extra two, three or four days that might have been required to complete the operation and I doubt whether the financial factor was decisive. (We have often been in worse straits since.) Last and least was Bulganin's rocket-rattling in a letter sent to Eden as late as 5th November.

Eden's comments are revealing on two grounds: they show the degree of illusion under which he was labouring and the degree of evasion to which he was prepared to resort in his own defence. He regards Dulles' actions at the United Nations as unbalanced, and his resolution of 2nd November as putting peace 'in a strait-jacket'. Where was *he* putting peace at that moment? On 3rd November he described the Anglo-French adventure misleadingly to the House as a 'police action' to stop the hostilities threatening the canal. In fact the Israeli-Egyptian war was almost over. The canal itself had been blocked and put out of action by Nasser, and our oil supplies had already been cut off. He comments that the Egyptian government 'was bedraggled in authority by humiliating defeats'. This was a complete misjudgment. Owing precisely to the Anglo-French intervention Nasser was able to convince his people that they had not been defeated by the Israelis. By 1958 he was back on his old aggressive tack, and eleven years after Suez he plunged into another round against Israel. Eden was so far from seeing his own posture objectively in world opinion that he accused Nasser of 'imperialism'.

The rest of the world had not stood still during these happenings. In Poland there were signs of restlessness; and above all in Hungary demonstrations had broken out on 22nd October which led to an insurrection against the government and a demand for the withdrawal of Soviet troops. The Soviet response was to strengthen their grip and put down all disturbances with decisive force. They also on 2nd November vetoed Eden's attempt to get action from the Security Council to restrain them. So at the very moment when Britain and France were helping Israel to attack Egypt Eden attempted to get 'the rule of law' enforced against the Soviet government who, whatever the truth of their claim that the new Hungarian government had asked them to intervene, objectively wielded the force to turn down flat any possible intervention by the United Nations. Eden remembers sadly that the US representative on the Security Council voiced his suspicion that we were trying to divert attention from Suez. Many representatives considered that it was a case of the pot calling the kettle black. Eden could not understand how Nehru and his representative preferred both Nasser's and Bulganin's explanations of affairs to his own.

His sources of consolation were unworthy. A London bus-driver wrote to Lady Eden that eighty per cent of the crowd who demonstrated on 4th November 'were of foreign extraction, so that was no true census of opinion and can be ignored'. First, I was there and the bus-driver was mistaken. Secondly, how could he have judged the percentage anyway? Thirdly, how sad that the great diplomat should have to descend in his crisis to scorn of foreigners. Then Eden comments that the habits of the House, so turbulent throughout these days and weeks, had deteriorated. So of course had his. He was easily rattled, put off his stroke, reduced to saying that he did not really know when it was true only part of the time. He quotes, too, the revered but ancient – ninety years old – Dr Gilbert Murray who wrote giving the reasons why, in his dotage, he thought Eden's policy might well prove the only road to success. Eden comments that he agreed with the old chap. His colleagues, he says, observed that he was calm under the strain. If so, it is not what Nutting and others have observed since. 'I felt at ease. I was convinced that our course was the only acceptable one. That makes for calm.' That was not the impression of his top officials any more than of his Cabinet colleagues. The majority of the Conservative Party in the House remained firmly loyal. 'There are always weak sisters in any crisis.' That refers to two of his youngest and brightest colleagues, Anthony Nutting and Sir Edward Boyle, who, with Sir Walter Monckton, were the only ministers to resign on grounds of conscience. He admits that the general public was not so loyal. He foresaw that another Western intervention in the Middle East would be 'inevitable' – a favourite and loose word – within a year or two and expected as of November 1956 to be in office to deal with it. Others who were loyal were the French and Israeli allies in their acceptance of the cease-fire. This was a misunderstanding of their reluctant consent under pressure, and the longer-term effects were going to be severe. He repeats that Nasser's position was threatened, of which there was no sign in practice, and speculates that even Soviet 'entry into the lists' might not have saved him. He saved himself without it. He reckons that at least five more days' campaigning would have been necessary to occupy the whole canal. Good authorities, and lesser people involved like myself, doubt this very much. The Anglo-French attack moved the United Nations to action – as if that had been the original purpose – and was surely better than inertia. But the one method that Eden refused to contemplate was diplomacy. The President made it clear yet again that he thoroughly disapproved of his 'eighteenth-century tactics' instead of recourse to diplomacy and UN procedures. While much of the British Press blamed Dulles for the fiasco this did not worry him at all, and his reputation in his own country grew in stature. For Eden the fact that the two outside powers who took it on themselves to intervene in the Middle Eastern conflict were the two colonialists is of course coincidental. Finally, the old refrain: 'I had seen the chain of failure in the 1930s from Manchuria to Danzig.' Though that chain of failure was totally irrelevant, he had certainly added to it here.

The balance sheet of the Suez adventure is not difficult to draw up. Eden spoke a great deal throughout of preserving the sanctity of agreements. In practice he directly flouted the United Nations, and the 1954 treaty with Egypt. He equally flouted the Tripartite Declaration 'to resist any attempt to change the existing frontiers between Israel and the Arab States by force of arms'. He spoke much of his pro-Americanism: he managed to alienate the Americans to a degree never achieved before or since. He united them with the Russians for the first time ever on a major cause. He boasted of being a life-long Francophile. But he smashed the entente cordiale and by his behaviour helped to disillusion the French and ensure the return to power of General de Gaulle, with all that that has meant for us since. His haughty remoteness towards his Israeli allies did nothing to endear him, or us, to them. He set out to topple Nasser and strengthened his position. He proposed to calm down the Middle East by separating Israel and Egypt but his actions led directly to the mounting tension which culminated in the second six-days-war of 1967 and the continuing dangerous situation there today. He aimed at preserving our supplies of Middle East oil and succeeded in stopping the flow completely for a while. He went in to keep the canal open and it was closed for months. He imposed a considerable strain on the morale of the British nation, and not least on that small section of it which was responsible for its diplomacy and which was made to look silly all round the world. He exposed the expeditionary force to ridicule and to the snipers' bullets for nearly two months. As for the thousands of British subjects in Egypt, they were thrown on Nasser's mercy. I have seen an excited Egyptian crowd on the rampage, and they are capable of anything. The crowds were not let loose. Sir Humphrey Trevelyan maintained his dignity, and thus Nasser's respect, throughout and greatly helped to steady the position.

It was by now too late for Eden to see anything in perspective. As the US ambassador Aldrich pithily put it: 'Eden was ill and seemed incapable of coping with the situation.' On 6th November Eden spoke on the telephone to Eisenhower who was cock-a-hoop over his great victory – due largely to his firm stand for peace – and pleased to hear of the cease-fire. Eden jumped to the conclusion that all would be immediately forgiven and forgotten. The truth was quite different. The US government could never forgive or forget our corkscrew diplomacy so long as Eden was in power and our forces in Egypt. He found them harsher than before. He telegraphed to the President another short lecture on the dangers of Soviet penetration and Anglo-US disunity in the Middle East, and asked whether he could visit him in Washington in the next few days. The President replied that this must await the withdrawal of the Anglo-French forces which he trusted would take place immediately. Eden would not agree to withdraw until the United Nations emergency force had arrived. It began to arrive on 15th November;

but our leisurely retirement lasted another five weeks, until 22nd December. Eisenhower meant what he said; he had been tricked too often. By Christmas there was no point in his seeing Eden, and he never did. The Egyptian government, whose diplomacy through the whole crisis and its aftermath was probably the cleverest of the lot, came bouncing rapidly back, too. The canal could have been cleared without delay, but they declined to allow a start on it, and the Secretary-General of the UN, Mr Hammarskjöld, endorsed this, until the expeditionary force had gone. This cost us a few more millions of dollars for our oil. The US government withheld co-operation at any level until we had purged our guilt. In the intelligence fraternity we noticed that the head CIA representative in London, a retired admiral who was agreeable but not all that sharp, was smartly removed, no doubt because he had not reported effectively on his allies. He was replaced by a very tough operator with the brief that he should keep a closer watch on us in future. It seemed to Eden that in the United Nations Nasser was trying to dictate terms as if he were the victor. The bitter truth is that to a large extent he was. Who else was, if not he? Israel had made some temporary gains and won a period of relief. The United Nations had proved effective, for the time being. The Americans were all the more irritated by what they considered our stalling on various resolutions. Nasser bided his time, accepted help from wherever it was offered, and was back on top of the Arab world within a couple of years. The British and French forces, tails between legs, went back whence they came.

Poor Eden had to retire too, and on doctor's orders went off to Jamaica for a few weeks on 23rd November. This personal retreat caused extreme uneasiness amongst his colleagues, and shocked Churchill for one. Rab Butler, the eternal number two, took charge. As soon as Eden returned on 14th December he made a speech which showed how completely out of touch with reality he was by now. 'There is now a growing understanding in the US about the action

159

which Britain and France were compelled [*sic*] to take in the Middle East. I am sure that this will go on increasing. Does anyone suppose that there would have been a United Nations force but for British and French action? Of course not.' This *ex post facto* rationalisation was fantastic. The expenditure of some one hundred million pounds, the weakening pound, petrol rationing and the rest were thus designated as part of a plan to get a UN force temporarily into Egypt. 'It would have been easy to do nothing, but it would have been fatal, as in the years between the wars. . . . Russia supplied arms in such quantities because she knew the Egyptian dictator's ambitions suited her own book. The aim was just this – more satellites, but this time in the Middle East.' The truth was just this: there was never any danger or probability of any such thing. And finally: 'I am more convinced than I have been about anything in all my public life that my colleagues and I were right in the judgments and decisions we took.' On the same day Dulles remarked to Lloyd in Paris that our actions had caused 'revulsion' throughout the United States. Eden threw a crumb of praise to the French for their harmonious co-operation and added that there was no recrimination, political or military, either then or later. This is simply untrue. The French were furious at the time, and said so. As to 'later', it seems to overlook the existence and actions of General de Gaulle.

Eden's final pronouncements before resigning on 9th January 1957 were equally off the beam. Writing three years later he says roundly that 'Suez was a short-term emergency operation which succeeded'. In his comments on the simultaneous intervention in 1958 by the US in Lebanon and Britain in Jordan to save them from Nasserite infiltration he ignores the fact that in each case the country's government asked us to step in, which was hardly so with Nasser and Suez. I happened to be with the Chief of the Secret Service in his office when a junior came in with firm intelligence that Nasser would take action in Jordan within a matter of days. He added conscientiously that we could not use the information because it might reveal our source. (I have since wondered whether it was Philby, who was in those parts at the time and showed knowledge of these developments.) He was hustled out of the room and our intelligence was urgently passed on to King Hussein who had confirmatory information and asked us to act instantly. We sent in a very small force – in fact for some hours it was, by mistake, limited to one stout-hearted brigadier – and stability was restored. That was effective diplomacy. Suez was not.

On broader themes Eden voiced the opinion in 1960 that the period of effectiveness of the nuclear deterrent was passing. This has not been confirmed. He makes some more criticisms of the UN on the grounds that it is ineffectual and prone to condone breaches of international agreements. As to the former point it is true that the basis of the UN could well be re-examined and remodelled since the super-structure has changed so much in its twenty years of life. As to the latter, no international agreements can be eternally valid in these fast-moving days, and if the UN condone alterations favourable to the have-not nations they should be applauded. But Eden remains faithful to his theme: 'It is all so much more difficult to do later on, and so we come full circle. The insidious appeal of appeasement leads to a deadly reckoning.' He thus equates appeasement with diplomacy. There are all too many instances to justify the view. But the conclusion should be to work out a sounder and more forward-looking diplomacy.

In his final message on television he repeated that the difference between the West and Egypt was not colonialism but that between democracies and a dictatorship. Certainly the most powerful democracy in the West, the United States, did not think so. He himself, he said, was the same seeker after peace and justice as he had been in the 1930s. It was all too true that his mind and outlook seemed to have stuck there. The tired voice referred, with a pseudo-Italian accent, to the 'Fusheests'; what a contrast with Churchill's manhandling of French and robust 'Nahzis'. In diplomacy, as in other forms of business, if you act on false analogies with the past you will produce the wrong answers. The diplomacy of the 1930s was disastrous anyway and led to the Second World War. It was the diplomacy of war, under Churchill's control, that got a move on. Its methods were not applicable to the post-war period; but a gentle relapse into, as far as possible, the style of the 1930s was no more suitable. And so Eden could never understand that, while he was condemning the 'morality' of the Soviet intervention in Hungary, most of world opinion was equally strongly condemning the 'morality' of Suez. He could never understand, or even believe, that many nations and their leaders saw him as a latter-day Mussolini, rather than condemning Nasser as a dictator. The wheel had indeed come full circle, but not as Eden conceived it. For after deceiving friends, colleagues, allies and peoples Eden had finally come round to deceiving himself.

THIRTEEN

The Aftermath

WORDS LIKE 'trauma' and 'watershed' are often bandied about in connexion with Suez. The use of such fancy metaphors is suspect and suggests embarrassed and unclear thinking.

Certainly Suez was a shock to the British people. The question is whether it was a big enough shock. Resilience is one thing; euphoria is another. The equal shock to the French led them soon to take novel and far-reaching measures. The Americans, less intimately concerned but greatly shaken all the same, did their best to quell their suspicions of their allies. We British tried to carry on in the world as if nothing had happened.

In the FO the under-secretaries, after raising a well-bred eyebrow at the unseemly demonstrations on 4th November, welcomed the gradual return to more normal diplomacy in which they could play their usual methodical part. The routine had been only temporarily shaken. Some conservative-minded officials were not above alluding to the Labour opposition's legitimate activities as 'a stab in the back'. Kirkpatrick received a GCB to add to his GCMG. Dean got his K a few months later. Since then he has been a good ambassador to the United Nations and to the US government, both of which he had in the course of duty helped to hoodwink throughout the Suez affair. I was promoted to be the youngest minister in the service and given an honour.

Macmillan took over as Prime Minister, as he had planned, and Butler stayed in his usual place. Lloyd remained, remarkably enough, at the FO. He also became leader of the House he had deceived. Nutting had resigned, and Dodds-Parker and the two other junior FO ministers, who had shown some indignation over their shabby treatment, were hustled out. Neither Nutting nor Dodds-Parker ever held office again.

There is no doubt that the majority of the Cabinet and of the Conservative Party had supported the Suez adventure throughout. This was partly because they were not informed of the degree of deception of our allies which it involved. Partly too it came from the traditional desire to show that the 'lion still had teeth', to 'teach the wogs a lesson', and so on. A year later the high Tory Antony Head, though he had been removed from the government by Macmillan, could still make some staunch remarks in the House. Eden, he said, had seen the menace of Communist infiltration to 'the backward countries'. He had seen the risk that this country would 'go down the slippery slope of infiltration'. The Suez operation was 'circumscribed by geography. . . . The operation is now regarded as a failure. Why? (Honourable Members: 'Because it failed.') In my view Sir Anthony Eden was absolutely right in his decision.'

Well, Head as Minister of Defence at the time of the operation knew the full facts. But Eden was in fact right in thinking that the majority of men in the street backed the venture, for the same mixture of reasons. The Trafalgar Square demonstration showed that a vociferous opposition existed, but in the turmoil of those critical days, and with the sombre distraction of Hungary, not too many people kept their thinking clear. Certainly a great majority, including myself, considered that since the laboriously mounted expedition had got as far as it did it should have finished the job. Even Dulles did. The further away people were from Eden the more they tended to sympathise with him and even admire him. Anyway when he collapsed he was succeeded by what appeared to be exactly the same kind of old Etonian gentleman with exactly the same kind of Cabinet. The public did not enjoy petrol rationing but they of course blamed Nasser and the Arab oil states for it. So much for the 'trauma'. As for the 'watershed', the adventure and its failure proved to some that Britain was no longer fit for the 'send a gunboat' stint. Most people drew no particular conclusions except that we had had bad luck and that, unaccountably, several of our best friends had failed us. Most people agreed with Eden's poor view of the United Nations and thought it ridiculous that the principle of 'one nation, one vote' should apply where the discrepancy in wealth and power was so great. These were of course the same people who would have resisted to the death any suggestion that a poor and uninfluential individual should have a less powerful vote in his or her own parliamentary elections than the richer minority. A thinking minority saw that the Suez effort exemplified British and French slowness of reaction to a situation which had in fact existed since we got ourselves into the war in 1939, and in pronounced form since we emerged from it in 1945 bereft of empire and of the power to control it. This was the final fling before we acknowledged that there were two super-powers in the world. In reality they had been there for a dozen years.

But, nothing daunted, Macmillan met Eisenhower and Dulles in Bermuda in March and they were most magnanimous to him. They and many other American diplomats had always preferred him to Eden. It looked as if the 'special relationship' was restored. The Suez Canal was cleared and run efficiently by the Egyptians, which Eden and others had said was impossible, and in a few months it appeared that our position in the Middle East was undented. Trevelyan duly returned from Cairo and found that as a result of his frank and critical attitude to the Suez venture ministers were too busy to see him. The Queen however was not. He was much tempted to leave the service. It is lucky for British diplomacy that he did not. He is the outstanding career diplomat of his generation and things might have developed better if he had been appointed Permanent Under-

Secretary of the FO instead of the conventionally minded Hoyer Millar and Caccia.

To the government, and certainly to the people, it seemed like business as usual, and diplomacy too. That proved to be the root of the trouble to come.

FOURTEEN

After Eden

WITH EDEN OUT of the way British diplomacy appeared to perk up a bit. But the basis remained the same and there was no one with the insight, the courage, the power and the time to remedy matters. Dean Acheson's apophthegm has been boringly often quoted, but it is none the less true for that: Britain had lost an empire and not yet found a role. She was 'just about played out'.

Selwyn Lloyd remained as a routine Foreign Secretary but Macmillan in fact took over the reins from Eden's hands. He was a far more astute politician and a more widely experienced man of the world. One of his Chancellors, Peter Thorneycroft, has said that politically he enjoyed living on the edge of bankruptcy. Certainly his style was more *dégagé* than Eden's and he was capable of original and sensible initiatives. He could and did frequently confer with the President of the US on a friendly basis, which Eden had been unable to do. He was prepared to visit Black Africa and the Soviet Union, and to promote efforts to get us into the Common Market. But our economy refused to flourish. Our professional diplomats conducted affairs just as before. Our forces remained scattered aimlessly and expensively all over the place. You can play about on the brink of bankruptcy for only so long. Then the creditors close in, and it is too late for the old style of living – and diplomacy.

Macmillan's Bermuda meeting with Eisenhower in March 1957 went almost too well. In the Press and in the FO the idea was put around that we were back in our special relationship with the US. This was, in the first place, a dangerous illusion, and it is never profitable to base diplomacy on illusions. The Americans were growing mightily in power all the time while we were diminishing; the relationship could not be, and was not, special in the old sense. As a matter of fact it never had been since the war. Secondly, the spectacle of our lolling back on this cushion was irritating to many people in Europe and beyond, and some took measures to let us down with a bump. It was of course essential to restore good relations with the US first of all. But we had wasted so much time and energy over Suez that we were now lagging in other directions.

On 25th March, the day after the Bermuda meetings ended, the Six signed the Rome treaties setting up the Common Market and Euratom. The US government had pressed us ever since the war to get much closer to Western Europe. But the FO had no serious idea of the economic importance of the step and preferred to carry on with political, military and commercial agreements and contacts in the traditional style. To the Commonwealth Relations and Colonial Offices it was unthinkable that the empire should not come first, or even that imperial interests could possibly be reconciled with what is loosely called our 'entry into Europe'. Eden refused to consider seriously any advance in that direction; he was embarrassed by friendly approaches from our West European allies. Churchill was more forward-looking but devoted only sporadic efforts to the question. So the powerful European Economic Community came into being on 1st January 1958 and has made solid advances since then, even if it is in some disarray at the present.

Macmillan had taken charge so forcefully that he felt no need to go to the country until October 1959. When he did he assured the voting public, as a patrician speaking the argot, that they had 'never had it so good'. This was strictly true, and for that matter is even true today. But it was grossly misleading. While our general standard of living improved over the years in a lethargic way, economic miracles were taking place in such countries as West Germany, France, Japan, to say nothing of the US and the USSR. We were going better than before but still slipping back in the race. And so when we delivered our riposte, in the shape of the European Free Trade Association, it was nothing marvellous. It did not get moving until May 1960, and was by no means of comparable economic strength or political importance. However, it gave some Whitehall officials the opportunity of jesting about Europe being at sixes and sevens. It became increasingly apparent even to the FO that a combination of the two was required if Western Europe was to deploy her full strength and that it was for Britain to bridge the gap. But it was not until November 1961 that negotiations were begun. Under Edward Heath's leadership we proceeded hamhandedly. One of his chief lieutenants in the negotiations, Sir Pierson Dixon, was given the impossible task of being ambassador in Paris at the same time. Our attitude throughout was that we were doing the Six an honour and that they must amend the Rome Treaty to suit us. They however, and in particular the man who was by now President of France, saw matters quite differently. The British public were told little of the true significance of the negotiations, and always in a boring way. Heath did his best but got bogged down in arguments about tariffs on canned kangaroo tails from Australia. At Nassau in December 1962 President Kennedy and Macmillan ganged up, in de Gaulle's eyes, to produce the bribe of the Polaris missile for France. De Gaulle had, and has to this day, never forgiven the Americans and British for rescuing France in the World War; and the stain on France's honour as a result of the Anglo-French Suez fiasco was vivid in his mind. When Macmillan, acting as Kennedy's messenger-boy, hustled over from Jamaica to Paris in January 1963 with the offer of the Polaris de Gaulle told him where he could put it. And on the question of Britain's entry into the Common Market he pronounced a resounding *non*, the first of a long series that so far shows no sign of ending. The British negotiators were astounded, incredulous, hurt. Surely they had done all they could and should? De Gaulle must be out of his mind.

In the Middle East too our diplomacy proceeded on traditional lines as if nothing special had happened. Here again our influence and interests appeared to prosper none too badly. However they were declining all the time compared with those of the US and the USSR. In March 1957 an up-to-date version of the Truman doctrine, this time named after Eisenhower, provided for US forces to protect the independence of Middle Eastern states, and the mighty US Sixth Fleet – units of which had 'accidentally' got in the way of the Anglo-French armada approaching Port Said in 1956 – confirmed its presence in a big way. The Bagdad Pact states ended their token boycott of Britain, and the Suez Canal was functioning smoothly by April. So was the resilient President Nasser who was working in all possible ways, including terrorism, to dislodge the ruling pro-Western elements in Iraq and Jordan. 1958 was a triumphant year for him, and it was a direct backlash of the Suez venture. In February Egypt and Syria proclaimed their union as the United Arab Republic under Nasser. Iraq under Nuri-es Said and Jordan under King Hussein formed the rival Arab Federation. This was too much for revolutionary and anti-Western Arab circles everywhere and on 14th July Nuri-es-Said, King Feisal and numerous supporters were murdered in Bagdad. So would our ambassador, Sir Michael Wright, have been if an Iraqi soldier had not missed him at three paces.

I had been since October 1956 Foreign Office Adviser to the Chief of the Secret Service, Sir Dick White, and we had received plenty of intelligence pointing towards this violence and indeed towards the assassination of King Hussein. Unfortunately we had no precise information on dates; possibly the assassins themselves made up their minds only at the last moment. However the Americans and we were able, as I have described, to forestall a clean sweep of the board by Nasser thanks to our immediate intervention in

170

Lebanon and Jordan. King Hussein was now out on a limb. Nasser broke relations with him and signed a military treaty with the new government in Iraq. Greatest triumph of all, he received the promise of a loan from the Soviet government for building the Aswan Dam. In Eden's phrase, the wheel had indeed come full circle. All these developments resulted from the Suez escapade and our failure to learn its lessons. And there was more to come in the same strain, much more. In Cyprus, too, we were in a fine mess and the killing rose to a climax in late 1958. A good move, however, had put the liberal-minded and astute Sir Hugh Foot in as governor in place of the unimaginative Field-Marshal Lord Harding, and also the whippy and ingenious Major-General Kenneth Darling instead of the cumbersome Major-General Kendrew. I was lucky in that when I arrived to take up my post as minister with the Middle East High Command just before Christmas 1958 the violence was in its last throes. Making the peace with Archbishop Makarios was wearing to the nerves but at least it was not explosive to the body.

In Europe the Foreign Office tried once again with our Western allies to arrange for German reunification after free elections, and naturally received the same *nyet* as before. A far more imaginative suggestion came from the Polish Foreign Minister, Rapacki. This was a plan for the gradual demilitarisation of both parts of Germany plus Poland, Hungary and Czechoslovakia, as a prelude to political discussions on Germany in the more relaxed atmosphere that would thus have been created. This appealed to a good many of the British opposition, including Hugh Gaitskell, but not to our traditionalist diplomats. I later included it in my plan of 1962 for taking the heat out of the German, and particularly Berlin, situations, and the plan had a favourable reception in personal talks I had with members of the government of the German Democratic Republic in 1964. It has still got nowhere in the West. Also in 1957 Britain exploded her first H bomb, and was not quite sure what to do with it. More significant, the USSR launched her first sputniks, or 'fellow-travellers', and served notice on the world that she could deliver her H bombs anywhere and everywhere. The year ended with a Soviet government suggestion for a summit meeting which the West did not welcome enthusiastically.

In 1958 the effervescence provoked everywhere in the Middle East by Nasser extended to Aden, where a state of emergency had to be declared in May. I was rushed out at a moment's notice for consultation with the Governor, Sir William Luce. Nothing noteworthy came of our discussions though for the first time a CIA representative was brought directly in on our Aden problems. It was to take us nearly ten years, and cost us many lives, to realise that what was required was not a build-up of our forces there but their removal. The Governor and I had a narrow escape not from the terrorists' bullets but from a giant sting-ray that got into His Excellency's reserved part of the sea when we were swimming there. (Or perhaps the creature was a Nasserite agent in a special disguise.) Earlier in the year I had had a most enjoyable and instructive trip round the world of a kind never promoted before or since: I visited numerous posts in Asia on behalf of both the FO and the Secret Intelligence Service, and conferred with the CIA representatives there. They received me everywhere most kindly, not least when I stayed with CINCPAC in Pearl Harbor. The quiet-spoken Admiral Stump, who had the power to blast any country in the world out of the water, was a most courteous host. With him as with the CIA men in Asia I was freely given access to the details of the CIA's intelligence gathering and operational methods and scope, including a plan for disrupting President Soekarno's Indonesia as a step towards removing him. This has now been achieved. The power of the CIA was impressive, but they collaborated readily with the representatives of our infinitely more modest SIS. The climax of my trip was a large lunch given me in Washington by Allen Dulles, Foster's brother and the Head of the CIA. They constituted a powerful family partnership. I was able to see for myself that in the intelligence world at any rate the treachery of Maclean and Philby, and Eden's offensive policy over Suez, had not permanently harmed our close relations with our American colleagues.

In March 1958 Khrushchev displaced Bulganin and took over power on his own. For the next six years there was to be never a dull moment in world diplomacy. All the more so as General de Gaulle became President of France in December and Castro Premier of Cuba a couple of months later. Britain proceeded as before with our Cabinet, and also our Foreign Office and Diplomatic Service, firmly based on the principles and methods inculcated at Eton and Christ Church, and the like. If Khrushchev's behaviour in banging the rostrum at the United Nations with his shoe seemed ungentlemanly to many people in the West, equally numbers of our political and diplomatic representatives looked like quaint survivals from the nineteenth century, or even caricatures, to the new men from the Communist countries, Africa and Asia.

Khrushchev began the hotting-up process by suggesting a summit conference again, which the West again declined. All that came of this was a very long Foreign Ministers' conference in Geneva from May to August which went endlessly and repetitively over the old German ground. For the first time at such a conference a representative of the GDR was allowed to attend as an observer. This was Herr Bolz, their Foreign Minister, who later told me a tale illustrating Gromyko's pawky sense of humour. The Western delegates were always at pains to pretend that the GDR did not exist: it was 'the so-called GDR'. Towards the end of one meeting Gromyko excused himself 'as I have to have so-called lunch with the so-called Herr Bolz'. The French ambassador in Bonn jested similarly when apologising for being late for a meeting with us allied representatives in Berlin a couple of years later. 'Unfortunately as I motored through the so-called GDR my car collided with a so-called tree.' But joking apart, with this lack of realism on the Western side it was natural that no progress was made, and that the temperamental Khrushchev was irritated. But meanwhile Macmillan had showed initiative by visiting Khrushchev in Moscow, wearing a smart white fur hat, and by following up with visits to de Gaulle, Adenauer and Eisenhower. Where Eden had regarded the wily old Chancellor with admiration and even affection, Macmillan was far more wary. The fact that Adenauer lectured him about his visit to Moscow did not endear him to Macmillan, who had no intention of making British policy dependent on West Germany. Just to remind the West how exposed was their position in Berlin Khrushchev ordered the first buzzing of a US aircraft by Soviet jets in the narrow air corridor from West Germany. We were to get used to this nuisance as a daily occurrence when I was minister in Berlin in 1961 and 1962.

Meanwhile an even longer negotiation in Cyprus had begun to bring results. On the day when I arrived, shortly before Christmas 1958, the atmosphere was electric. Governor Hugh Foot had to decide whether to exercise his prerogative of mercy in favour of two convicted EOKA murderers. After much heart-searching and telephonic consultation with Macmillan in London he did so. This led to the early end of terrorism, as the terrorists were on the run anyway. It also created the atmosphere in which a preliminary agreement on Cyprus' independence could be signed in London in February 1959 between Britain, Turkey and Greece, and the crafty Archbishop Makarios could be allowed to return triumphantly to Cyprus from exile shortly after. Whether the relaxation of justice for political ends is ever a good thing in the long run is however another matter; and the endemic lawlessness of Cyprus ever since may provide a comment on the question. In any case the Governor, the Commanders-in-Chief and I then went into negotiations with Makarios which culminated in the independence of Cyprus and of the British Sovereign Base Areas only in August 1960. No detail was too small for Makarios to question: what price did the NAAFI pay for returned beer bottles, or charge for a packet of cigarettes, and so on. Each time we put forward a reasoned figure for the area we should need to keep for our bases he put forward another ridiculously low one.

However, we were prepared for these tactics; and we had the oriental bargaining skill of Julian Amery to help us. He was the man who came to dinner, so to speak, from the Colonial Office, and stayed three months. So we exaggerated our needs a bit, and matched every tiny concession by Makarios with an equally tiny one on our side. At one point when Makarios was being particularly infuriating I suggested to Hugh Foot that a little intercommunal bloodletting now might be all for the best in the long run. He replied that I was 'a hard and ruthless man'. So the bloodshed was postponed, though not for long. At the end of the negotiations the necessary base areas were safeguarded, and this part of the agreement has worked well ever since. But 'independence' was a misnomer for Cyprus, since the agreements stipulated the conditions on which Greece and Turkey could intervene to help their mutually hostile communities. We did not improve matters by indulging in a ridiculous bit of Whitehall warfare. It was clear to all that the continuing problem of Cyprus would be one of diplomacy between Britain, Turkey and Greece with which a FO character would be best equipped to deal. By now I held full ambassadorial rank and I volunteered to move the seventy miles up the road from Episkopi to Nicosia. I was however turned down (for which I thanked God subsequently) because Cyprus had opted to stay in the Commonwealth and our man must consequently come from the Commonwealth Relations Office, splendidly equipped with knowledge and experience of the problems of Australasia, central Africa and so on. Equally, in this faction-torn island the MI6 man, who had provided much useful intelligence, was immediately removed because gentlemen of the Commonwealth do not spy on one another. According to CRO custom an MI5 man was substituted to work in liaison with the Cyprus government, which meant, more and more as time went on, to exchange with the Greek Cypriot members of it tittle-tattle of very little use to the British representative in the performance of his diplomatic duties. This kind of thing still goes on today at many of our diplomatic missions.

In January 1960 Macmillan took another praiseworthy initiative. He was fortified by a friendly visit paid to him in August 1959 by President Eisenhower, and still more by the overall Conservative majority of a hundred in the elections in October. EFTA, such as it was, had got going. He turned his attention to Africa, where developments of portentous significance were on the move. The process of the British and French colonies becoming independent had begun and the speed was growing. An ever larger proportion of UN members came from that continent. The Union of South Africa was about to become an independent republic and leave the Commonwealth, as she did in 1961. Our Commonwealth Secretary ever since Eden came to power was the 14th Earl of Home. He was not an unkindly man but he had not the faintest idea of what was really going on in Africa and Asia, and he made no great effort to find out for himself. He was not at ease with black or brown men. He criticised the UN on Eden's lines: it applied a double standard. He could not grasp that in reality a double standard of living and everything else existed, that it was the responsibility of the developed countries to help the underdeveloped rather than to guard their privileges, and that countries like Britain should not expect tearful gratitude every time they acted on these lines.

Macmillan, who at his best was a good diplomat because he faced facts, had a far more sophisticated approach both on the emerging countries and on the UN. In January and February 1960 he visited Ghana, Nigeria and the Union of South Africa amongst other countries. In the Cape Town parliament he made his seminal 'wind of change' speech. It did not please his hosts and it astounded some of his Tory colleagues. It brought hope to many emerging countries, tempered however by the reflexion that it was out of character for a Conservative Prime Minister and a British diplomat. Macmillan had not only told a significant truth but also looked towards the future. The follow-up may have been slow and disappointing in many ways. But credit is due to Macmillan for this piece of original diplomacy.

In May 1960 Khrushchev got his summit meeting in Paris with Eisenhower, Macmillian and de Gaulle. He chose to make an instant fiasco of it by complaining violently about the American U2 spy aircraft which had been shot down over the Urals a few days before. He must have been astonished when Eisenhower admitted to the flight, since in the intelligence world it is customary to deny responsibility for such things by saying, for example, that the pilot must have gone accidentally a thousand miles off course, or mistaken the Urals for the Himalayas, or what have you. Anyway absolutely nothing was achieved at the summit.

In July 1960 Lord Home was made Foreign Secretary. His diplomacy was in every way similar to Eden's. On appeasement it was worse than Eden's. He had been actively on Chamberlain's side in favour of it, as his private secretary, where Eden had only gone along with him and then not till the end. But this was a small difference compared with the similarity of birth, background, education and general outlook. An hereditary millionaire, Home had naturally enough not the faintest grasp of the importance of economic and commercial factors in diplomacy, and light-heartedly admitted as much. His heart was never in the approach to the EEC. He was embarrassed by behaviour on the part of, say, Khrushchev or some black man at the United Nations that did not tally with the tenets of the British aristocracy. He could not get on close terms with American politicians and diplomats. He was often praised for his 'integrity', which as we all know is a quality supposed to be possessed only by the upper classes. It also implies that he stuck to an unimaginative continuation of Eden-style diplomacy. It was cosy there, in the FO, with all his fellow-Etonian acolytes around him. But out in the great world it almost came to thermonuclear war twice during Home's incumbency, over Berlin and Cuba; and the influence that conventional British diplomacy could exert in either case was minimal.

In November 1960 John F Kennedy was elected President of the US by a tiny majority over Richard Nixon, and in fact no overall majority if the half-million votes for minor candidates are reckoned in. Nevertheless his arrival was hailed as the beginning of a new epoch in which the US would advance to a new frontier. By now Khrushchev was laying about him right and left. Every few months he would produce an 'ultimatum' demanding that the Western allies quit Berlin and agree to settle the German question on his terms. He lectured the UN violently on colonialism, disarmament and whatever else came into his head. Kennedy, in his early middle age, was greeted as a sort of golden boy after the series of elderly presidents who had gone before, rather as Eden had been greeted on first becoming Foreign Secretary in 1935. Right, thought Khrushchev, we'll test the nerve of this golden boy. And Kennedy's first two years were amongst the most dangerous the world has ever experienced.

They began abysmally for Kennedy. The CIA had been hard at work on subversion of the new Castro régime in Cuba and were preparing, with Eisenhower's approval, a plan for the invasion of the country. Kennedy gave his approval too, and the result was the fiasco of the Bay of Pigs. That round went easily to Castro and the Communists, but Khrushchev was furious that the invasion had been attempted. He determined to have a personal confrontation with the new President and travelled as far as Vienna for the purpose where Kennedy met him in the course of a European tour which included Paris and London. At the Vienna meeting Khrushchev was very tough indeed. On Germany he gave Kennedy and his Western friends six months to sort themselves out. If they did not agree to his proposals by then, so much the worse for them. He would make a peace treaty with the GDR and establish Berlin as a 'free' city, access to which would be controlled by the GDR. Kennedy was shaken.

At that moment I had just learnt that I was to be transferred to Berlin as minister there. I paid a farewell visit to Government House in Nicosia. The lawns were as green and neat as ever; the Cyprus police band, in their English-style blue uniforms, played Gilbert and Sullivan. Only the incumbent was a bit different from his predecessors, for he wore a stovepipe hat and long black robes. President Makarios and I parted most amicably, and I flew off to London to be briefed.

Brief was the word. Everyone dealing with Germany was certain that something horrible was going to happen but uncertain what it would be. Although therefore my post would probably be a critical one important people were too busy to give me much guidance. Lord Home granted me about five minutes, his deputy Mr Heath about six. Then I was thrown in at the deep end. The atmosphere in Berlin in July 1961 was sultry and ominous. Khrushchev's latest ultimatum had an almost panic effect on people in East Berlin and the GDR. They got out in their thousands across the open frontier in Berlin while the going was good. By the second half of July the weekly total of refugees had reached four figures and for the next four weeks it swelled continuously. They all had to be screened because the Communist authorities slipped in a fair number of their agents. Our machinery creaked and groaned. Then, long before daybreak on Sunday, 13th August, the flow was stopped. The building of the Berlin Wall had begun.

The Wall, which we now know to have had a generally beneficial and calming effect in Central Europe, drove the Western allies almost hysterical. It seems probable that Ulbricht got permission from Khrushchev to go ahead only at the last minute. Our intelligence was accordingly not to blame for not reporting the decision. But it is extraordinary that with our massive combined resources – and not least our numerous German agents – no reports had reached us of the movement and stockpiling of hundreds of tons of material required for the Wall. The operation showed considerable skill in this direction. So the Western allies were in some disarray. We three ministers together with the three commandants and, when summoned later by us, Governing Mayor Willi Brandt, discussed the outrage for most of that Sunday – beginning at the amazingly early hour of 10 am – and tried to elaborate counter-measures. The US Commandant favoured a military advance by our tiny operational force through the embryonic obstacle. But there was the little matter of twenty-two Red Army divisions, with their jets, encircling Berlin. Had we advanced, we should then have had to retreat, unless NATO were to try to break through a hundred and ten miles of GDR to relieve us, with a strong likelihood of World War Three as a result. A couple of months later the US Commandant, heavily reinforced by the return of the Berliners' hero of the airlift days, General Lucius D Clay, had his way and carried out a token intrusion into East Berlin. That led to the US-Soviet tank confrontation and a new peak of tension. But on 13th August the best that we and our governments could devise was a stiff note of protest to the Soviet government. From that point on it was a question of 'how I learnt to stop worrying and love the Wall'.

Or rather, not from that point, although the die was then cast, but from a couple of years or so later. Throughout my year in Berlin the city's problems were headline news in the world Press practically every day of every week. On four occasions we officials were told – though quite rightly the publics in the Western allied countries were not – that Kennedy was contemplating all-out nuclear war to deal with the Communists' constant provocations. Khrushchev was testing him all right, almost to breaking point. The British and French generally counselled patience, but their views had no great effect on the President's decisions. Nevertheless a useful move was the appointment as British ambassador in Washington of Sir David Ormsby Gore in October 1961. He had been a good Minister of State in the FO and at the

UN and was a man of original and modern thinking. Also he was a close personal friend of the President and other members of the Kennedy family. This non-career appointment meant that at a most dangerous time we had a man who, unlike Makins and Caccia before him and Dean afterwards, could exert a personal influence greater than Britain's diplomatic standing objectively warranted. We can hope that the forceful John Freeman may prove equally effective. Both he and Ormsby Gore are Privy Councillors, like Lord Caradon (formerly Hugh Foot) at the UN and this gives them added weight with the government and a direct line to the Prime Minister. Before the war the top half-dozen career ambassadors customarily held the same honour, but this is never the case today.

In the same critical month of August Britain applied for membership of the EEC. The prelude was scarcely favourable as it consisted of Selwyn Lloyd's emergency budget imposing a wages pause and raising the bank rate from five to seven per cent. Perhaps this was meant as one of our sporadic attempts to show the world that, though we were in a mess, we meant business and would tighten our belts, etc. Unfortunately what has invariably followed on such occasions is that our friends are impressed more by the desperate nature of the situation which compels such measures, and let me add by the speed with which we loosen our belts on an ever more middle-aged paunch, than they are by the stern gestures. But Edward Heath and his team duly cranked up on their uninspired, uninspiring and mishandled round of negotiations. Heath's own official title was no help. Instead of being called Deputy Foreign Secretary, which he was and which would have been comprehensible to his European colleagues, he was Lord Privy Seal. So he had to explain, time and again, that he was not a Lord; and while no one took him for a lavatory or a performing circus animal, the whole bit of nonsense smacked of ancient insularity and was strictly counter-productive.

In Berlin we continued to have murderous incidents at

the Wall, sonic booms produced daily by Soviet jets, the buzzing of civil aircraft in the access corridors, and so on. In May 1961 George Blake, who had operated happily for the Russians in Berlin under the guise of our own principal spy there, had been convicted and sentenced to forty-two years in prison. So that particular activity of ours, formerly so flourishing in and from Berlin, was a goner. It impinged on me with increasing force that the Western allies were out on a limb here; that the GDR would tend to settle down and even flourish now that the main escape-hole had been bolted; and that, while the West should most certainly not abandon their hard-won position in Berlin, there would have to be new and improved ways of maintaining it. I naturally did not discuss such ideas with the Berlin Governing Mayor or his colleagues; they were not in my brief from the FO and were purely my own. I had some talk about them with my own staff and with a delegation from the Imperial Defence College on their annual visit. And then in June, just when I was going on my first long leave for two years, I was summarily removed from my post and retired from the Service. I was forty-nine.

This happening had considerable publicity over the following months. I was coldly informed by the head of administration in the FO that they did not intend to wash dirty linen in public; and as I for my part had none to wash I decided to fight the case. *The Observer* took up the cudgels on my behalf, and so did the Labour opposition. I made the FO withdraw a libellous indictment which they sent to me for my comments. Humphrey Trevelyan had advised me to cut my losses and not to attempt to keep a place in the Service, and I took his advice. The mills of the FO ground on, and at one stage approval for my retirement was sought from three retired officials including Sir Harold Nicolson, in his late seventies and, as everyone knew, senile. Hugh Gaitskell was most sympathetic and put Anthony Greenwood on to handling my case. I went to hear myself debated in the House of Commons. Greenwood and Harold Wilson made mincemeat of poor Peter Thomas, a Minister of State at the FO who had been put up to wield the hatchet. He had begged Greenwood not to persevere, but to no avail. His two high FO advisers, doleful men who looked uncommonly like Laurel and Hardy, were pale as sheets at the other end of the chamber. They have both gone on to be ambassadors, but Thomas failed at the next election and has been rejected as a candidate several times since. Greenwood next elicited by a series of pointed parliamentary questions addressed to Prime Minister Macmillan that I was not accused of being a security risk, a homosexual, a drunk, an embezzler of public funds, a Don Juan, or indeed anything particularly heinous. I had not collaborated satisfactorily with the major-general who was Commandant in Berlin, that was all. Naturally, few people believed the story. The *New Statesman* thought it more probable that my standing up to Chancellor Adenauer one evening in Berlin when he was being offensive and dictatorial might have earned me a black mark or two with our ambassador in Bonn, a close friend of his. Lord Home, under pressure in the House of Lords and oozing 'integrity' at every pore, agreed to re-examine the case. We heard no more of that. The FO's public relations were lamentable throughout. When I related my experiences in a book published in 1963 they became jittery and tried to hamstring the book by action behind the scenes. It nevertheless had some influence not only here but in the US, Europe, including Eastern Europe, and the Middle East. And my friends inside the FO tell me that as a result of the fright which the authorities got from the case some necessary reforms were introduced, notably in the direction of treating their officials as human beings. That is something important.

Berlin went on rumbling, as it does to this day. But two other trouble spots were pressing their claims in the danger stakes, one slowly but even more massively and the other explosively. In Vietnam Kennedy began the escalation which has since led us to within hailing distance of the brink. One of his close advisers, a top CIA man who was based in the White

House but who spent much of his time trying to make sensible arrangements with the South Vietnamese leaders, is a friend of mine and I have great respect for his judgment. He has always been a dove rather than a hawk. Nevertheless he thought the initial escalation, and the US mode of interference in South Vietnamese politics, were right. He collected a series of heart attacks as a result of the strain. Perhaps the nightmare illustrates how different is the US's situation from ours. With them there is the possibility, realised in the other crisis, of a matching of power and diplomacy; the danger is that the power cuts loose and the diplomacy goes by the board. With us diplomacy should and could usefully supplement our relative lack of power. In our case the danger is a different one: we tend to believe that conventional diplomacy can actually substitute for power, and thus we fool ourselves but nobody else.

The October crisis over Cuba was Khrushchev's last and greatest try-on aimed at testing Kennedy's nerve. Kennedy played it just right, and in the upshot he and Khrushchev were set to collaborate fruitfully if toughly. On 22nd October Kennedy announced in a broadcast the installation of Soviet missile bases in Cuba. My CIA friend from the White House flew to London to show the photographic evidence to Macmillan and to the Labour leaders. Kennedy's Cabinet of whizz-kids from business and the top university strata thrashed out the options, in the most subtle detail, by night and by day. Ambassador Ormsby Gore was treated almost as a member of that Cabinet and gave much wise advice. I was asked on the BBC when the crisis was at its tensest whether I thought nuclear war could be avoided, and I expressed the opinion that it could if the Soviet government were allowed just the right amount of room for manœuvre – not too little, not too much. I did not think that questions of face came into it much with them. They had always preferred hard realism to that sort of thing, even when it meant a temporary retreat. Kennedy judged it to a T, and was able to announce on 2nd November that the Russians had begun to dismantle their Cuban bases. If he had been spared for more than a year a very special relationship might well have been established between him and the Soviet government.

The formalities concerning my retirement were completed shortly before this and I immediately gave *The Observer* a long article on Germany to which they gave top billing in September and which caused quite a stir. I expressed the view that the Western allies' lack of realism and general policy of waffle had had its day and was now dangerous to all. I proposed a package deal. The Oder-Neisse frontier should be recognised without more ado because it existed and would continue to exist. The same went for the GDR. West Berlin should become an independent entity with its access routes guaranteed by the four wartime allies and the GDR, and with the usual right to invite troops of friendly powers to be stationed on its soil. All three parts of Germany should be members of the UN; to this day not one is. A major UN agency, such as the Human Rights Commission, should transfer its headquarters to West Berlin. The Warsaw Pact and NATO governments should discuss seriously changes on the lines suggested in the Rapacki plan, that is the demilitarisation of Central Europe. In these ways a *détente* could be brought about which was not only desirable in itself but which would offer the best hope of eventually uniting Germany. I was quite clear that the Western policy of banging its head against the Wall and then protesting because it was there would get us nowhere. These views annoyed many of my ex-colleagues in the FO, as I expected. It is so much less trouble to lean on a reliable old *status quo* – until the deathwatch beetle gets into it.

It was not only President Kennedy who grew to full stature in 1962 but also President de Gaulle. With great political and personal courage – feelings ran so high that there was more than one assassination attempt – he pushed through the independence of Algeria against powerful opposition. This was an essential move both because Algeria was ready for independence and because the situation there had been bleeding away France's strength for too long. Then a pattern for his future behaviour and policy was set when the French representative declined to attend the eighteen-power conference on disarmament at Geneva. De Gaulle was of course planning his own nuclear *force de frappe*. Outside the de Gaulle pattern was the Anglo-French agreement in November to develop the Concorde aircraft. I expressed the view then, and will again today, that this is a nonsensical venture. The cost already bears no relation to the original estimate or to any favourable results in the commercial or political sphere. Delivery dates have already slipped heavily and will slip more. Instead of already flying at 1400 mph as promised it has so far achieved 15 mph on the runway. The proud boast that it would fly years before its US or Soviet counterparts is likely to go the way of so many such boasts. Indeed it is fair to ask: will it ever fly at all commercially? In January 1963 de Gaulle lashed out in two directions. He delivered his massive rebuff to Britain on the Common Market question, in sorrow at our inadequacy just as much as in anger at our blundering diplomacy. And he crystallised his senile love-affair with Adenauer in the Franco-German treaty of co-operation. For good measure he began withdrawing French forces from NATO in June. Thus, thanks largely to de Gaulle, Britain had gained the Polaris missile at the cost of her exclusion from the Common Market and the disruption of NATO.

In June agreement was reached on the White House-Kremlin hot line, of major importance both practically and symbolically. This cemented the US's only 'special relationship' today, that with the USSR. Another important result of the new Kennedy-Khrushchev relationship was the signing in Geneva on 5th August of the partial nuclear test ban treaty between the US, USSR and Britain. We were not in a position to take the initiative but rightly went along with it. The treaty was later signed by ninety-six countries but not, of course, France or China. Meanwhile however conditions were growing steadily worse in Vietnam and

Kennedy's feet were firmly set on the escalation ladder. At the end of 1963 a great many upheavals happened almost at once. In October Ludwig Erhard was at last permitted by the eighty-seven-year-old Adenauer to succeed him as Chancellor, but Adenauer beavered away in the background to make sure that he should fail. Macmillan's health collapsed and, after a Conservative conference where half a dozen leaders nakedly scrambled for power while Macleod demurely remarked that British gentlemen are above competing with each other, Butler emerged in his usual place and, incredibly for this day and age, the Earl of Home on top. Macmillan's lavish farewell distribution of honours to his personal staff – a peerage, a baronetcy, a knighthood and so on – was in marked contrast to Eden's rather mean dole-out in 1957. A few days later world turmoil was increased by the assassination of President Diem of Vietnam, in which the CIA were rumoured to have taken a hand. But none of these events mattered one iota beside the assassination of President Kennedy on 22nd November. Not only millions of American hearts bled on that day but millions of Russian hearts too and of others all round the world.

It seemed like the end of an epoch that had hardly begun. Not that Kennedy's diplomacy had achieved all that much; and what he had achieved was done dangerously. But he had devised a modern method of diplomacy based on the hard facts of relative political, economic and military strengths and, equally important, on the actual and potential changes in the balance as they came along. The chief change to come concerned China, who for years had become more aggressively independent of the USSR and who into the bargain exploded her first atomic bomb in October 1964. In the same month Kennedy's friend Khrushchev was replaced by the level-headed, managerial types Brezhnev and Kosygin. All logic pointed to a rapprochement between the US and the USSR, and in some ways this developed. But there was the ever more blood-filled gulf of Vietnam between;

there were the persistent dangers and differences in the Middle East; there was Berlin. Would Kennedy and Khrushchev together have coped better? That is for some ingenious novelist to say. And while these gales of change were raging in the high places of the world Britain, her economy and her diplomacy went down, and on the whole painlessly.

The Middle East was quiescent after Nasser was stopped in his tracks in 1958. Syria pulled out of the United Arab Republic as early as September 1961 but, given that she is endemically the most restless Middle Eastern state bar Cyprus, remained on generally good terms with Nasser all the same. Arab hatred of Israel remained as deep as ever. Incendiary speeches were made from time to time in Egypt, Syria and other Arab countries, and it was clear that another in the series of explosions was bound to come sooner or later. All this stemmed from the British handling of the situation at the end of the mandate and during 1956. Up to January 1963 Kim Philby, while enjoying the *dolce vita* of Beirut as a part-time journalist and part-time SIS employee, was also devoting his real energies to promoting the sort of confusion in the Middle East which suited the Soviet government and which might in the long run make the West's huge oil investments less secure than they might appear. On this point the Americans had always had the sense to see that straight commercial profit was what weighed most with the oil-producing countries and that the maintenance of Western armed forces in the area was not only unnecessary but counter-productive. The British were slow to learn this lesson. In January Philby departed to his spiritual homeland, the USSR, after being convicted by Blake's confessions of being a Soviet spy for many years and inexplicably allowed to go by the MI6 men who had their fingers on him. He undoubtedly left a good stay-behind organisation.

In December 1963 the uneasy situation in Cyprus cracked and intercommunal warfare broke out as heartily as it had a few years before. Three months later, in March 1964, a UN peace force went in under the Indian General Gyani since matters were getting ugly. It has had a roughish time and has not been able to stabilise the situation to this day. A week after its arrival Makarios made certain that the position would get worse by unilaterally 'abrogating' the 1960 treaty between Turkey, Greece and Cyprus, which he had not the faintest right to do. Under international law Cyprus now had no government since the Turkish Cypriots declined to collaborate as the constitution provided. That remains the position today. The turbulent prelate also overlooked the geographical fact that Anatolia is very near indeed to Cyprus, though the Turkish jets reminded him from time to time. An unhappy, though beautiful, island. The British diplomatic contribution was twofold. Under a series of efficient air marshals the Sovereign Base Areas kept themselves to themselves and provided calm and remunerative employment for tens of thousands of Cypriots. While in Nicosia, under the aegis of the Commonwealth Relations Office, one ineffectual High Commissioner succeeded another. It needed only the tiresome General Grivas, aged about seventy by now, to return as he did in August 1964 to try to revive the terrorist glories of EOKA. Turkey and Greece, allies in NATO, were now on the verge of war and Greece withdrew some of her forces from NATO. The British had bequeathed this mess in Cyprus and could do nothing about it. Rather more constructive was one of Khrushchev's last great acts in neighbouring Egypt, where in May 1964 he officially opened the Aswan Dam.

In central Europe too the situation was quiescent, though Khrushchev reminded the West from time to time that they were out on a limb in Berlin and that he might chip at that limb from time to time. I was writing a good deal about the Berlin and German problems in the Press and I decided that the time had come to see the GDR properly, since my occasional trips when minister in Berlin had usually been official and had never taken me beyond East Berlin. The Rector of Humboldt University in East Berlin invited my wife and myself to come for as long as we liked, and to go where we liked, as the University's guests. The hospitality everywhere was admirable, the discussions wide and free. I talked with several Cabinet ministers including the head of the Christian Democratic Union, and was told that 'the McDermott plan' would be acceptable to the government of the GDR as a basis for negotiation, which meant that it would be acceptable to the Soviet government too. No attempt was made to exploit my visit. A brief communiqué, which I had approved, was the only public report. The British right-wing papers were far more jittery. One rang up a friend of mine who is now a Cabinet minister and suggested that I might be 'doing a Maclean' (after all, our names begin similarly). My friend said he thought they would be unwise to run that line. Another, in a column run by a licensed buffoon, used an incorrect report to indulge in some near-libel. I returned with the strong impression that the GDR not only existed but was flourishing economically now that the Wall had settled matters down. At the same time I had indicated clearly to my East German friends how repugnant I found many aspects of Communism, and not least the custom of shooting at escapers near the Wall. Matters are considerably improved in this respect today. I have since been cordially invited to return to the GDR and I look forward to doing so before long.

After thirteen years of Conservative rule Britain was in the worst financial and economic mess ever, and as always this was crippling her diplomacy. In the closing days Douglas-Home had exaggerated the Eden-Macmillan attitude of being *au-dessus de la mêlée* in economic matters, and had not only done his sums with matchsticks but considered that the nation would be amused to know that he did. Here is that 'specific levity' at work once more. The Labour Party was elected back to power in October 1964 but with an overall majority of only five. Their first task was to deal with a trade deficit of nearly eight hundred million pounds. On the same day Khrushchev was replaced, in a more dignified manner than the Conservative Scarborough scuffle of 1963, by

Brezhnev and Kosygin. The next day China exploded her atomic bomb. On 3rd November President Johnson won a sweeping electoral victory to continue in the post he had taken over willy-nilly a year before. In Rhodesia the ominous Ian Smith had become premier in April and he now held a referendum which yielded a ninety per cent vote in favour of independence. A friend of mine on the High Commissioner's staff in Salisbury had reported from the moment Smith took over that the man was a tricky and treacherous type who would use any means to achieve his own and his gang's ends, including the cynical claim that they were more loyal subjects of the Queen than the members of Her Majesty's Government. These reports disappeared into the maw of the Commonwealth and Foreign Offices, and no action was taken until it was too late.

Labour supporters had hoped that amongst other more basic things a Labour government would give a new and modern style and method to our diplomacy in place of the superannuated Eden style which had for so long been inappropriate. The conditions, both at home and abroad, were none too favourable. Let us look at the balance sheet over the four years since October 1964.

FIFTEEN

Diplomacy Yesterday and Today

INTERNATIONAL RELATIONS NEVER stand still, even for a day. Nations, like families in private life, are constantly on the move either up or down the power scale. Some who appear most stable are having to run their hardest to stay where they are. Diplomacy can be skilful or unskilful. But in any case it begins at home and depends on the home base. As communications, in all senses of the word, become more rapid and pervasive – and this has been an outstanding development of the last thirty years – so the old-style diplomacy becomes swiftly less effective.

Harold Wilson's choice of Foreign Secretary in October 1964 was not inspiring. Patrick Gordon Walker is a perfectly conventional upper-class public schoolboy and he contrived to be defeated twice in rapid succession in the election of October 1964 and a by-election in January 1965. He then retired hurt and was succeeded by Michael Stewart. It was not until George Brown's brief reign began in August 1967 that anything like a jerk was put into the Foreign Office. However, two good, and unconventional, ambassadorial appointments were made. Sir Hugh Foot, who had courageously resigned from Patrick Dean's staff at the UN over the principles of our policy on Rhodesia, was now made a Minister of State at the FO and Lord Caradon, and he supplanted his former head of mission in New York. For the first time since the UN came into existence British policy was based on the reality that over a hundred and twenty nations existed with equal rights in the General Assembly; and that the UN was not, as Eden and Home had expected it to be, in any way a body elaborately devised to further British interests. Then John Freeman, an attractive character and a tough journalist and television performer, was sent to India with whose problems he was known to have the deepest sympathy. If he could achieve practically nothing there it was not his fault but that of the situations of Britain and India in the world today. He certainly held the fort as well as any British ambassador could. It is to be hoped that he will take his own independent line in Washington. He has easily dealt with the mischief-makers who suggested that because he expressed criticism of Nixon some years ago he will be unable to get on terms with the new Nixon in 1969. As a result of the 1964 report of the Plowden committee on British representation abroad – the first committee from outside the FO which that department had ever allowed to examine it – a few timid organisational steps in the right direction were taken. HM Diplomatic Service, which Eden had abolished in his democratising zeal, was revived and at last the Commonwealth service was amalgamated into it. Incredibly, three separate departments in Whitehall still continued to run our overseas affairs, though this has at last been rationalised in 1968. I had written articles recommending most of the Plowden reforms, and others more far-reaching, some time before the report appeared. But of course the entire style and personnel of the diplomatic service, and particularly the upper reaches, remained exactly as before: major public school, particularly Eton and Winchester, and Oxbridge. When Old Etonian Caccia retired as Permanent Under-Secretary in 1965, Old Etonian Gore-Booth duly succeeded him. So it was largely a distinction without a difference.

But all this professional diplomacy was not in any case the nub of the question, which was that Britain's financial and economic position had to be repaired as quickly as possible. This depended first on the people who work, from the factory hand to the chairman of ICI. Secondly it depended on a government with such a tiny majority that it had to move in a more gingerly fashion than it would have liked, and which faced an opposition unwilling to recognise that their divine right to govern had been taken from them and none too scrupulous about ways and means of getting back on top. Traditionally the left talk a lot about class warfare; the right however go smack in and wage it. Eden after Suez reflected ruefully that when Labour take energetic action abroad they always have the full nation behind them, whereas any Conservative Government's initiatives will be regularly sabotaged by the Labour opposition. This is a looking-glass world indeed. Representatives of the Conservatives in opposition, such as Salisbury, Sandys and Douglas-Home, have shown a readiness to denigrate our elected government when visiting, for instance, Rhodesia that has sometimes fallen not far short of treason. People like them prate most of empire and Commonwealth; they have done most to bring about the Commonwealth's disintegration. If we cannot overcome the Avery Brundage syndrome – he is the octogenarian American millionaire who, as chairman for thirty-five years of the Olympic Games organising committee, did his damndest to bring the Union of South Africa back into the 1968 games at the cost of offending half the world – it will be the fire next time in Britain and elsewhere; and soon. The omission from our international cricket team for the tour of South Africa of undoubtedly our best all-rounder, Basil D'Oliveira, because although a British subject his 'Cape Coloured' origin would not please the South African authorities, is an outstanding case of racialism. The decision was taken by Douglas-Home, amongst others, as an MCC committee member, and was publicly greeted with acclamation by South African ministers and others devoted to apartheid. The belated and lily-livered reversal of the decision has in every way made matters worse. And thus we have reached the position of taking orders from Mr Vorster.

Harold Wilson's first problem was to cope with the pressure on the pound which had resulted from the Conservatives' mismanagement, and already in November 1964 foreign bankers showed their confidence by granting a large loan of three thousand million dollars. A few days later he went to see President Johnson in Washington and established a good relationship, so much so that on a subsequent visit Johnson compared him in a speech with Churchill. This sound collaboration, in which Wilson recognised that the finery of the 'special relationship' was a thing of the past, has paid off. The US government are relieved that we no longer display pretensions to equality, or even superiority, of standing and judgment such as Eden and Home embarrassingly and thoughtlessly displayed. They prefer dealing with contemporary human beings such as Wilson and Brown rather than with aristocratic left-overs. They had high hopes of a Labour government. They have shown great sympathy over its difficulties and expressed it in a solid financial way. In return they are prepared to listen to our political and diplomatic advice, even over such terrible problems as Vietnam, though naturally they are not prepared to be guided by it one hundred per cent. Why on earth should they be? Wilson in due course established another sound relationship with Kosygin.

In Labour's first five hundred days there was little time to spare for important diplomatic initiatives other than those connected with remedying our parlous economic situation. Thus when India, which over recent years seems bent on suicide, embroiled itself in a senseless, bitter little war with Pakistan over nothing at all, it was Kosygin who brought it to an end, and not the ex-governors of the Raj. Similarly in 1962 the US and the USSR had combined to stop the Chinese attack on India, a fruitful collaboration which Chinese propaganda has exploited ever since as one example of the USSR's collusion with the imperialists. As regards India, I wonder seriously whether a dose of Communism (quite apart from Kerala) is not what she needs. I have seen Communism at first hand more than most people and I hold no brief at all for it in Europe. But in the corrupt conditions imposed and consistently maintained by the ruling caste in India it might really be the answer. Her government's boast that she is the largest democracy in the world is a mockery of the word. Ask her millions of untouchables what they think about it.

In September 1965 we arranged for further massive support for the pound from the central banks. In November Ian Smith, a couple of weeks after talks with Wilson in Salisbury, made his Unilateral Declaration of Independence. His régime was declared illegal, and in spite of our difficult economic position we introduced stiff trade restrictions. The Archbishop of Canterbury and the leader of the Liberal Party declared that the right thing might be to use force, and at that comparatively early stage it might indeed have solved the problem less bloodily than it will probably be solved in due course. To my own knowledge two or three members of the Cabinet favoured it. At any rate nine African states who favoured it broke off diplomatic relations with Britain in protest at our weakness. One Commonwealth state, Tanzania, has only recently resumed them.

In February 1966 Minister of Defence Denis Healey announced the first big steps in the rationalisation of our defence policy and equipment. We were to leave Aden by 1968 and our aircraft carriers were to be phased out over five years or so. For the first time since the war an effort was being made to get our priorities right. Previously Defence Ministers had enjoyed far too much independence both of our economic and of our foreign policy. Stupid squabbles between the three forces had regularly led to wasteful expenditure on a large scale. Our forces had been distributed all over the world as if we were still the world's policeman. In Asia they were regarded as useful by the governments concerned because of the money they spent and the work with which they provided the inhabitants, who also enjoyed venting their spleen on them from time to time. As an instrument of empire they had become anachronistic and counter-productive. There is no empire any more. The Labour government has been working out what commitments we can no longer afford and withdrawing men and equipment accordingly. Thus it was no longer diplomatically necessary to deploy forces 'east of Suez', to use that neo-Kiplingesque phrase. Equally the TSR2 was a load of expensive rubbish which it was right to cancel. I was told personally by the number two Air Chief Marshal in the RAF that he welcomed the cancellation. The RAF would have enjoyed flying the F111A, of course. But we cannot afford it and they are not repining at the cancellation of the order, especially in view of the bugs with which it seems to be infested.

The people of Britain liked what they had seen of the new government and were not impressed by the Tories in opposition under Heath. On 31st March 1966 they gave Labour a clear mandate with an overall majority of ninety-nine. Now, surely, was the moment for bold economic measures including the devaluation of the pound and statutory control of prices, wages, salaries and dividends for two years at least. The opportunity was muffed and these measures, which were unavoidable, were taken piecemeal and half-heartedly over the next two years. The worst might have been over by now; instead we are still in the thick of it. These hesitations have given the Communists ample room for their disruptive measures, and Philby and Blake in Moscow must have many a good laugh as they watch our economy floundering.

On 12th January President Johnson said in his State of the Nation speech that the US was strong enough to fight the cruel war in Vietnam, pursue its goals in the rest of the world, and build the Great Society at home, all without increasing taxes. He was wrong on every single count, and the accelerated escalation from then on has been the greatest stumbling-block in the way of all the US's most important objectives both nationally and internationally. It has aroused an unheard-of degree of protest in friendly countries, not to mention the Communist world. The Soviet government, while anxious for a rappochement with the US government, cannot let them off the hook in Vietnam. They must get off it by themselves. But in the long run the situation can only play into the hands of an aggressive, expansionist, nuclear-armed China. British diplomacy has done and is doing what little it can to ease the position. A government emissary in the shape of Harold Davies was sent to Hanoi to see his friend Ho Chi-Minh, an errand that was almost bound to be fruitless, which it proved; but worth trying all the same. Mr Wilson has acted when required as go-between with Mr Kosygin and to say the least this has not made matters any worse. While backing the US government in its determination to stop the Communists – and does anyone really think we should back Ho? – we have expressed disapproval of the bombing of North Vietnam and suggested to the US government from time to time ways in which they might mitigate the adverse effect of certain measures on world opinion. None of this is heroic diplomacy, which is very rare in any circumstances. But it is sensible and useful, and befits our role in the world.

Another form of escalation took place in 1966, this time fortunately of a serio-comic type. This was in the diplomatic and other activities of the ageing de Gaulle, who laid about him in all directions almost like a poor man's Khrushchev. In February he called for the dismantling of NATO and promised further French withdrawals from it. In March he told it to remove all its headquarters from France. In June he paid a state visit to the USSR, where his hosts pandered obligingly to his megalomania. He then went round the world in three weeks. Meanwhile the Minister of the Armed Forces, M Messmer, promised French nuclear-headed rockets by 1969: what might be called the 'force de crappe'. In September France virtually withdrew from NATO except for maintaining a liaison mission. De Gaulle then pronounced that the US must simply withdraw from Vietnam *sin más*. In December he gave Kosygin eight days' lavish entertainment in France and that gloomy man appeared almost light-hearted on occasions. At the end of March 1967 NATO and Supreme Headquarters Allied Powers, Europe, did as they were told and withdrew to Belgium. The first point about de Gaulle is that he is good for everyone, even for us over the Common Market. The second point is that nobody else takes him as seriously as he takes himself, and rightly so. His diplomacy is that of a past age. He tries to play off the two greatest powers, and various others, against each other; but he does not possess the basic resources to do it effectively. Naturally the Communists welcome his hostility to the US; but they do not over-estimate its practical effect. The same goes for his actions regarding NATO, which was showing signs of disintegrating in any case. It is important to keep our sense of proportion and humour about de Gaulle. It is not by chance that George Brown got on at least reasonably well with him while our solemn professional diplomats get nowhere. De Gaulle's collapse in May 1968 might have been foreseen. You cannot eat, sleep and live *la gloire*. And it seems almost certain that he nurtured a viper in his bosom, in the shape of a top minister in his Cabinet who was a Kremlin agent, out of obstinacy because the warning on the subject came from an American – President Kennedy. So while de Gaulle was away in Romania being glorious and telling the local government how to behave, the position blew up behind his back. And the Germans once again invaded France, led by Danny 'the Red' Cohn-Bendit. True, de Gaulle is still there. By the use of the thugs of the CRS, who were proud to be called the French SS, by far-reaching concessions on the industrial pay structure, and at a cost of hundreds of millions of pounds to the French economy, the old man has kept his place. It cannot be for long.

On the Common Market front de Gaulle has not only made a nuisance of himself to his partners but a bloody one to us. Wilson and Pompidou discussed the issue in July 1966 in London and Pompidou made the flat statement that nothing prevented our entry so long as we accepted the Treaty of Rome and the numerous arrangements subsequently agreed. A tall order for us; but fair enough. In August George Brown became Foreign Secretary and made it clear that we were determined to get in. Since then it has been *non, non et non* at intervals from the General. Is he not justified in many ways? Do the British behave like Europeans when they are on the continent? What about our drunken gangs loose on their day trips in Ostend or Calais? How many of us speak a single continental language respectably? Surely it was more sheer ignorance than British *pudeur* that caused even quite highbrow journalists to translate de Gaulle's memorable '*chienlit*' as 'dog's breakfast', as if it had something to do with '*chien*', rather than 'shitabed'? I hope so, though it is not encouraging either way. How many demand their cups of tea and chips in Pisa or Algarve? At home we are just beginning, timidly, to 'go metric'. The word 'continental' is still largely used as a dirty one, connoting either unbridled sex or – 'yet another accident at continental-type railway crossing' – disregard for safety. A large advertisement warns us that one family in three faces 'a ruined holiday abroad' because of diarrhoea caused by dirty foreigners. I have been behind the scenes at one of London's most expensive restaurants and I should without fail take my Entero-Vioform before eating there. Furthermore, we still drive on the wrong side of the road. We do not think the question of extended contacts important enough to justify more than an annual fifty pounds' travel allowance. For many of us the attitude is still that of the newspaper in the 1920s reporting a storm in the Channel: 'Continent cut off from Britain.' We have advanced a bit from the condescending attitude of Heath and his fellow-negotiators five years back. The members of the European Economic Community have advanced too, and in most ways faster. De Gaulle's opposition to our entry may have originated in prejudice and resentment over the past. But it is firmly based on facts today. Otherwise the other five could have overruled him – or shall we say four and a half as the Federal Republic of Germany is only half on our side. There is little doubt that we shall make it, eventually. But since we have shown so clearly how badly we need to, because there is so much in it for us, it stands to reason that we have first to prove we are in every way a desirable member, and that we must be ready to pay the price, which will be high both in basic adjustments of attitudes and for some time economically. The world does not owe us a living. And the Common Market emphatically does not owe us one of the highest standards of living in the world at the cost of any of its own well-established principles.

The end of 1966 was the beginning of a bad time for West Germany. The National Democratic [sic] Party under von Thadden won its first electoral victories in the province of Hesse. This is a purely Nazi party as anyone who has heard its leaders' speeches or read its newspapers can see for himself. Von Thadden demands, in speeches greeted with the old Nazi-style hysterical acclaim, the annexation by West Germany of the GDR, Austria, and parts of the USSR, Czechoslovakia, Poland and Italy. His newspaper is anti-semitic, while he himself has said unguardedly that there is no call for violent anti-semitism in West Germany simply because there are so few Jews left there. He declares that he looks forward to the new French H bomb being used to help West Germany. His party has gone from success to success and is likely to get between forty and sixty seats in the Bundestag elections in 1969. Everywhere except in the Communist world, and not least in Britain, people bend over backwards to protest that these National Democrats are not Nazis, and that history does not repeat itself. Myself, I hear the voice of the Old Adam and the screech of the butcherbird as clearly as Vansittart did in the 1930s. The West German government have refused to ban the party on the grounds of freedom of speech, though they banned the Communist Party in 1956. This is not surprising given the composition of the ruling 'Grand Coalition'. In November 1966 a floundering Erhard resigned as Chancellor and Willy Brandt had the chance of taking over, admittedly with a tiny majority such as both Kennedy and Wilson had obtained when they came to power. But true to the feeble Social Democratic tradition in German politics he jibbed. It would have been hard going, certainly, but it would have been lively and it would have meant that the democratic cut and thrust would have been preserved. As he refused ex-Nazi Kiesinger, head of the Christian Democratic Union, took over. There is no effective opposition any more. And the new Nazis flourish. Of course history does not repeat itself word by word. One of Eden's great faults was to compare Nasser with Hitler. No one in their senses would compare Kiesinger, ex-Nazi though he is, with Hitler. But history spirals; or, shall we say, it is a double helix. The German character seems to remain particularly constant over the generations. Similar manifestations appear at the different levels of the spiral. They could produce similar results to those in the past; similar, but even worse. But there is hope in the fact that the government and most of the people of the GDR, comprising nearly a quarter of the total count of Germans, are inexorably opposed to any Nazi-style, or even Axel Springer-style, adventures. They do not all love Ulbricht by any means. But they prefer him to Kiesinger, Strauss and, particularly, von Thadden.

There is still hope that West Germany may pull itself together. But the events leading up to the Middle Eastern six days' war of 5th–10th June and its aftermath suggest that the critical problems resulting from the British Palestine mandate and of the Anglo-French Suez adventure of 1956 are practically insoluble in the foreseeable future. Nasser was faithful to his word that the war against Israel would go on and on. Thanks to his successes in ordering the UN contingent out of the UAR and in blockading the Straits of Tiran he became over-confident, which his whole political history shows is his habit from time to time. The Israelis were fortunate in not having half-hearted allies this time, as they had in 1956. On their own they could finish the job swiftly and then hold hard. King Hussein's trip to Cairo on 29th May, and much advertised kissing of Nasser, who had so often tried to have him removed and even assassinated, made war certain. His ready collaboration in the Nasser lie, as Nasser himself has since acknowledged it, that US and British aircraft were helping the Israelis was not to his credit.

Well, his little kingdom is now smaller still and has no future. It will be surprising if he himself survives for long. However, the Arabs' mentality is a very special one, and no one in the Arab world thinks it particularly odd that not a single national leader fell as a result of the great defeat. Indeed, they do not see it as a great defeat but, in Nasser's words, as a mere setback. And taking the long view they may be right. Israel is in contravention of the UN's resolutions in holding on to her conquests, and her occasionally arrogant attitude has alienated even some of her friends. All efforts by the UN, the USSR and the US to stop the fighting were in vain until Israel chose to stop. This shows how ineffective the greatest powers can be in certain critical conditions.

The Arabs are now preparing for the next round and the familiar guerrillas, this time called Al Fatah, are again operating. It looks a hopeless prospect. The Arabs just do not want a peaceful solution; they want Israel dumped in the sea. Certainly the UAR's economy is hard hit by the closure of the Suez Canal, which clearly will never regain its old importance. Even the British, always so jittery about the canal, are managing perfectly well without it. The large subsidies which Nasser is receiving from his richer Arab allies will dry up before long, as is the custom in inter-Arab affairs. Only a complete change of heart on the Arab side can lead to a peaceful settlement, and it seems unlikely that this will occur without a further instalment of the twenty years' war. The Arab guerrillas keep the fires stoked under their various names: fedayeen – 'those who sacrifice themselves'; Al Assifa – 'storm troops'; Al Fatah – 'conquest'; Al Saiqa – 'thunderbolt'. The Soviet government might conceivably put a stop to it in due course, but for the present they prefer to keep the waters troubled and do some considerable fishing in them. So the short- and medium-term prospect in the Middle East is turbulence which neither the US nor the USSR will control. As for the long-term prospect, is is only possible to say that these two powers are no more likely to allow a third World War to start here than any-where else.

The highly favourable out-turn of the war for the USSR was that they can now sail a large warfleet up and down the Mediterranean, using UAR and Algerian ports, cheek by jowl with the US Sixth Fleet. One good result of the war was that Kosygin, during his visit to the UN, had long and friendly talks with President Johnson at Glassboro State College, New Jersey, on 23rd and 25th June. British diplomacy over all these developments was sensibly aimed at cooling the atmosphere. We displayed none of our traditional pretensions to being the paramount power in the Middle East. We had learnt that lesson. It was a wise move to use Sir Harold Beeley, a former ambassador in Cairo who had got on well with Nasser, to help repair relations as soon as was feasible. Beeley is no oil painting, has a twitch and a stammer, wears dowdy suits; but he treats Arabs as intelligent human beings and not as inferiors, which has been the tradition with too many British diplomats. His job is not made easier by blimps such as Lord Mancroft who saw fit to describe in the Lords the closure of the Suez Canal as 'a ridiculous farce', and to cast aspersions on the skill and honesty of an Egyptian dentist who operated on a British seaman from one of the ships bottled up in the canal. 'I should not like to put myself in the hands of any dentist of the UAR,' said his Jewish lordship. It is a state of mind. In similar vein it cannot help matters to refer in speeches and articles to the man who has been President of Egypt and the United Arab Republic for some years as 'Colonel Nasser', as people like the *Daily Telegraph*'s and *Daily Express*' reporters, or Quintin Hogg and Douglas-Home, are apt to do. Would he care to be called 'Lord Dunglass' today? However, the prize for the most inept comment on the affair must be awarded to the ageing Eden. Starting off with the hilarious words: 'If I had been Prime Minister now' (a sense of humour was never one of his strong points), he went on to say that the crisis took him back not eleven years, but thirty. He drew a strange and misleading analogy between Israel and Czechoslovakia. Nasser, of course, was Hitler. There you have it.

In Aden British and Arabs were getting killed with increasing frequency and futility. It was rightly decided to hasten the withdrawal. To negotiate this Sir Humphrey Trevelyan, who had retired from the Diplomatic Service after putting up the best performance for a generation by any British ambassador in Moscow, was recalled from his well-earned retirement. The former High Commissioner, a colonial governor called Sir Richard Turnbull, had treated a high-powered UN delegation as if they were a bunch of his subjects. Trevelyan displayed his usual courage and incisiveness, and the job was swiftly and successfully completed. Never has a life peerage been better earned than his. For many years our colonial governors in Aden, latterly disguised as High Commissioners, had paraded the Nasser takeover bogy as a reason for hanging on. For several years I for one had written that this takeover would not occur. Now that the inflated and anyway unnecessary Middle East Headquarters with all its trappings and forces has been removed there is hope of good, profitable relations. The maintenance of small forces in the Persian Gulf is a sop to our protected sheikhs, and to the traditionalists in the rump of the Colonial Office. The sooner they are withdrawn, and the sheikhs put out to cope with today's world, the better. Our relations with the Arabs and the Iranians will only benefit, above all in the most important sphere which is that of commerce.

SIXTEEN

Diplomacy Tomorrow

IT CANNOT BE said that British diplomacy has been brilliantly successful over the last generation. Can we do better? At least what John le Carré has called 'the thousand-year sleep of Eden and Macmillan' (I personally would give Macmillan credit for some waking hours) is over. The Foreign Office List, the annual red book that doggedly preserved to the last a section on protocol as laid down at the Vienna Congress of 1815, has recently given up the ghost. The dead hand of Harold Nicolson who, on the basis of a career ending when he was only a counsellor, laid down immutable principles of diplomacy harking inexorably back to the eighteenth century, has been removed and nobody reads him seriously any more. The fact that he was an intimate friend of Guy Burgess was in any case not encouraging. Lord Strang, with his bureaucratic starchiness, cannot be read with pleasure or benefit today. The routine memoirs of retired ambassadors in their sixties and seventies are invariably unreadable. We have no Murphys or Thayers or Kennans.

These however are the minutiae of the case. I believe that with some fundamental rethinking of the purposes of British diplomacy over the next ten years – it is no use planning further ahead in this day and age – and a basic retooling and jigging of the machinery we can achieve more both for ourselves and for the world at large. Indeed Wilson and Brown started the process, and it is a pity that the Brown epoch was so short. In considering the future it is logical to begin at the bottom or base, which is our national capability; to work through the machinery and methods of our diplomacy; on to the nature and feasibility of our objectives; and finally to the part we can and should play in the greatest world issues, and how best to play it.

Diplomacy in the classical style, as described by Nicolson and practised by Eden, Home and their FO supporters, lived a life of its own in a world of its own. You were, unofficially, expected to have private means to practise it effectively. You were not expected to know much about your own country, except the areas of it inhabited by the ruling few, as Sir David Kelly well called them. And the public fully supported this view. For them diplomacy was a portentous and esoteric matter which only the toffs could handle. In contrast, a left-wing MP asked the Prime Minister in the House recently whether we could not with advantage abolish the Diplomatic Service altogether. The answer is no, since diplomacy is required for the conduct of international business in certain spheres. 'Secret diplomacy', incidentally, of which Eden and his like spoke in reverential tones while others condemn it as a sort of sinister conspiracy, is no more than the confidential part of that business, necessary as in any business dealings. But the MP's question was not a bad one.

It all comes back to our economic potential and development. Foreigners are not fools, as has always been assumed in wide circles of our people. Those nations which are clearly more powerful and economically expansive than we – the Americans and the Russians – have an objective and shrewd assessment of our achievement and capability at any given time and they keep it up to date. The same applies to those who, in different ways, are mounting the ladder faster than we: the Japanese, the Common Market countries, and the Chinese. From a different angle the less prosperous countries watch us too. So it is no good our trying to throw about weight that we have not got. What we need is a realistic forecast of our economic development and then, based on that, a priority list of the diplomatic objectives on which we can profitably go to work. While the main priorities must be clear they must also be flexible since so many of the medium, and even some of the major, diplomatic developments are unpredictable. In making the economic forecast we should be wise to be pessimistic. How often we read that the production figures for a certain period would have been satisfactory if it had not been for various strikes, an embargo on something by an African country, the closing of a canal, or what have you. We should also be wise to subtract something from our more optimistic forecasters' figures for productivity, production, and the balance of payments. Over the last generation we have never achieved figures of this kind.

In a word, we should work out realistically what kind of diplomacy we can afford, and what are the machinery and methods best suited to our case. The official records admit to eleven thousand British diplomats of various grades and an annual expenditure of £86 million. In practice we can add ten per cent to both for various ancillary services. This does not include the cost of the Secret Service, officially given as £11 million but actually a good deal more, or of service attachés. Totting it all up £125 million would be a fair figure. This is a flea-bite compared with the still grossly inflated defence estimates at over £2000 million; but it is a pretty penny all the same, and a large number of staff, for a service whose product is largely shrouded in mystery against the public who pay for it. We keep up about a hundred missions abroad, headed by some fifty knights and other lesser personages. Top salaries are £8600 plus tax-free allowances in the five-figure bracket plus most luxurious living accommodation, most of it empty for most of the time, and such perks as lovely cheap drink and numerous other privileges. These embassies are like palaces, and from time to time we build a new one on a similar scale. In Brazil we have recently built two.

The tax-free allowances are called *frais de représentation*. But what are our ambassadors representing? Formally, the Queen; but nowadays what is more important is that they should represent contemporary Britain. Many of the grander ambassadors fail to do this, on two counts. First, it is hardly typical of our technological society to live in a palace surrounded by numerous servants. Secondly, as they come without exception from the Eton-Winchester-Oxbridge stable, have never done anything but diplomacy in their lives, and are almost without exception over fifty-five, the great majority are not in touch with everyday life and developments; and, understandably enough, they prefer it that way. As one of the Ministers of State at the FO remarked to me recently, with feeling, nearly all our ambassadors are unbearably square.

This is serious. Equally serious is the fact that in spite of efforts to attract a more representative cross-section to the FO, and Michael Stewart for one has taken some trouble over this, they obstinately decline to enter. There are various reasons for this. While the FO no longer has the glamour it had a generation ago it still looks pretty stuffy to most young people. At the top they see a collection of people who seem to belong to a past age and whom they have no desire to resemble. Although the perks are good young people are not all that much tempted by them today. They can earn bigger money, and travel just as freely, in other jobs. Then the intensity of the Buggins' turn syndrome is forbidding. At present you just cannot get into the top echelon before you are fifty, and it is very rare before you are fifty-five. Sir William Armstrong was number three in the Treasury when forty-three, head of it at forty-seven, and now at fifty-two is head of the entire Civil Service. No such career is possible in the FO, while in industry or journalism you can well be at or near the top in your late thirties or early forties. For instance, a recent advertisement for an appointment to the senior management of an international bank specifies: 'Initial basic salary will be negotiable over £10,000. Candidates should ideally be about forty.' It is no coincidence that Armstrong, within a few weeks of taking over his new job, has made two important public pronouncements. The fact that they are public is good for a start: a breath of fresh air to fan the hitherto faceless men. But, even better, they call for a shake-up of the Civil Service as a whole on the lines of the shake-up (and it was my word first!) of our diplomatic machinery and policy which I have recommended for some time now. Provost Leach of King's, Cambridge, admitted that he had his tongue in his cheek when he recommended in his Reith lectures that everyone should retire from every kind of responsible job at fifty-five. But examining the character and structure of the Diplomatic Service you begin to wonder whether it might not be a good thing. Certainly the recent press protests by Sir Nicholas Cheetham at being eased out at fifty-seven, and Sir Patrick Reilly at fifty-nine, are ridiculous, undignified and out of place. In any case most people are at their peak between about thirty-eight and fifty-three, and they should be deployed accordingly.

A shake-up is needed if the FO and Diplomatic Service are to grapple with contemporary problems. George Brown began it but left too soon. There were high hopes when he went to the Foreign Office as there had been of Eden thirty years before. He behaved like a human being and not like a stuffed shirt. Since most countries are represented by human beings today his style appealed to many. Equally he offended the stuffed shirts; and a good thing too. A bit tiddly on occasions? So what? I could name you a dozen ambassadors who make a habit of going to bed well lulled, shall we say, by the hard stuff at 10s 6d a bottle and the wine cheaper still. Brown hit it off well enough with both Presidents Johnson and de Gaulle. His junior staff liked him. One senior ambassador of the conventional type told me that he thought he might make a great Foreign Secretary. Alas – here again like Eden – he was difficult for his ministerial and senior officials to work with. However, he appointed a new Permanent Under-Secretary, Sir Denis Greenhill, who is the first man of that rank, anyway in the twentieth century, to have worked at something other than diplomacy: he was with the railways until he fought a gallant war and only joined the FO afterwards. Also, unlike his two Etonian predecessors, he went to a minor public school; and he has been given specially rapid promotion for the purpose. Whether he can made a breakthrough remains to be seen.

Some other immediate steps could and should be taken. Half a dozen of the top knights who are more fossilised than most should be summarily retired before the sacrosanct age of sixty to make way for younger men. It should be made clear to all that, as in the Navy, they are liable to be retired at about forty or about fifty if they do not appear to be keeping pace. All professional diplomats should be shunted out at least every six years for two or three years, to the city, industry or some other government department. A number of serious commercial and economic experts should be incorporated in the Foreign Office and trained up. Only a couple of years ago a young Oxford first in politics, philosophy and economics, after winning his way into the Foreign Office and asking to be given the economic work which was his forte, was roughly told that he would have to wait ten years for that. He resigned. It would do no harm to have a Permanent Under-Secretary or one of the half-dozen Deputy Under-Secretaries from the Home Civil Service. All other departments exchange staff in this way, but I can recollect only one such secondment during the past thirty years, from the Treasury and at the not very elevated level of Assistant Under-Secretary. Outstanding individuals should be promoted much faster. Capable outsiders should be brought in at all levels, either on short service or permanently. Women should be given a serious chance of rising to or near the top; so far mere lip service has been paid to this, and yet at certain posts and in certain conditions they could be more effective than men. The record shows some highly successful lady ambassadors from the Soviet Union, Morocco, Guatemala and Sweden. We are told that all such measures would undermine the morale of the service. If so, *tant pis* for the existing morale. It must be brittle. But in fact this is rubbish.

On the contrary it would create a new and more vigorous sort of morale, both positively and by leading to the disappearance of some of the stick-in-the-muds. On one occasion *The Observer* gave me some favourable publicity and I was rebuked from on high on the lines that 'the FO do not advertise'. I wonder why not? They might be better placed if they did.

Many of the same criticisms apply to the Secret Intelligence Service. Its importance is admittedly declining now that so much crucial intelligence is obtained either by satellites hundreds of miles up in the air or by electronic devices concealed in the fly-button, and so on. Nevertheless I think it is still worth preserving on balance, because in spite of the harm done to our information-gathering and policy by Philby, Blake and the rest the Service has pulled in a good few important traitors from the other side who have equally blown the Communists' efforts. But here again we are too gentlemanly. Philby, Maclean and Burgess were able to achieve what they did because of the old boy net, and it continues to inhibit the tougher form of security which is desirable. All the dozen top members of the Service, and several who have recently retired – some of them into the Diplomatic Service – were personal friends of Philby up to his escape to the USSR. And, curiously, half a dozen others have gone in for extreme right-wing politics. An ultra-conservative spy should surely be a contradiction in terms. Again, security of diplomatic cover is often lax, though we tried to tighten it up in my day. If you looked down the list of the diplomatic staff at, say, Beirut at any time a few years ago you would find amongst the comparatively junior First Secretaries one suddenly festooned with CMGs and other honours, sticking out like a sore thumb. It was not difficult for the enemy to guess who he was. So I insisted that the rank of Counsellor, where such honours are normal, should be opened to the SIS boys. Personally I would not mind one or two becoming heads of mission, as CIA staff sometimes do, but this has been considered too daring so far. We also abolished the seniority table in the front of the Foreign Office annual list since it was easy for a painstaking enemy to discover from the body of the work that some 'diplomats' were mysteriously omitted from it. This omission deprived a number of keeny-beaks of one of their principal pleasures, that of counting the months till probable promotion, always of course on the optimistic assumption that dear old Francis would get caught in the wrong bed once too often or lovable Ronald would drop dead. But the sacrifice was worth the reward in added security and the seniority table is now circulated only within the Service. It is not very encouraging that the newly appointed chief of the SIS is a lifelong diplomat of the usual education, stamp and age. Someone rougher is needed.

Numerous other measures are called for. First, a new head office is required. The St Pancras station exterior of the FO could be preserved at a pinch. But the interior is ridiculous. On the one hand there are the murals of a breasty Britannia and her colonial offspring; on the other the Locarno room is divided up into innumerable plywood cubby-holes. The lift stops less often in mid-progress than it used to do, infuriating the important ambassadors whom it imprisoned. But everything tends to smack of the horse and buggy age, and this is not conducive to sharp thinking and forward planning. We could take a leaf out of the GDR's book here. They have a completely modern and very impressive Foreign Ministry in Berlin. But I do not expect to live to see the day. Can you picture a giant computer whirring away next to Horse Guards Parade? They are used to good effect in the CIA's modern establishment at Foggy Bottom. And so they could be here not only on questions of adminstration but of security and even, to some extent, of policy. I can imagine a computer, properly fed with the facts, helping to produce a sounder and less amateurish policy than some of our hit-or-miss diplomats. Then it would have a good effect not only for candidates but for the oldies too, if required reading, included Herman Kahn on Thinking about the Unthinkable and On Thermonuclear War, together with Provost Leach.

Marshal McLuhan, too, has much to offer, as here: 'What do we know about the social and psychic energies that develop by electric fusion or implosion when literate individuals are suddenly gripped by an electromagnetic field, such as occurs in the new Common Market pressure in Europe?' What indeed? The most modern guides on cybernetics and computerisation should also be at every diplomat's fingertips. And he or she should be versed in the history and methods of the KGB, the CIA and the SIS.

Furthermore, the pecking order of our missions abroad should be seriously reviewed and kept constantly under review. At present the traditional order is preserved almost without exception. But with all respect to our allies and friends does Rome really deserve to be a grade one embassy today? Or Brussels and The Hague grade two? Today Lusaka really is more important than Vienna, and Havana than Madrid. To Saigon we have always appointed ambassadors of the most junior ranks possible, while the US government have sent representatives of the calibre of Mr Cabot Lodge. This has two immediate effects. Our ambassador can have practically no influence in his post. And the US government are bound to wonder whether we really take Vietnam problems seriously. But it is easier, of course, for our authorities to go on as before. It should have been apparent from the start, for instance, that except precedence-wise the Reillys were unsuitable for Paris. He is a very typical Old Wykehamist who would have made a good undersecretary at Housing or Trade, but who is totally unable to impinge on General de Gaulle or his ministers. Nor did he get on well with George Brown or the Press. It is true that he is being retired a few months early, but some time has been lost. What is needed as our ambassadorial couple in Paris is two chic, extrovert people who do not look or behave like officials, backed up by a capable number two who will do the donkey work. I have my doubts about Christopher Soames' suitability but none about his wife. It is a pity she was not made ambassador. By a curious coincidence, too, the more cushy posts have the largest staffs, whereas some of the tough, lively and less pleasant posts have less than they need. In Paris the senior staff consists of 39 civilians and 6 service attachés, while in Israel the figures are 12 and 3 respectively. In agreeable Stockholm there are 17 and 5; in critical Vietnam 16 and 4. And so on. A reshuffle is needed, with flexibility to follow. An overall cut of ten per cent, such as Lyndon Johnson recently imposed, would probably make for efficiency. For a start the number of service attachés should be drastically reduced. No mission needs more than one, least of all in friendly countries and particularly those where some of our forces are stationed, and in many cases one man could cover several countries. Then a cut in entertainment allowances would do no harm, and would save many an up and coming diplomat from the affliction so commonly found amongst elderly ambassadors, fallen arches due to an excessive number of cocktail parties.

Before leaving the machinery we should consider a final point leading on to the policy: what is a British diplomat, or perhaps what is he for, today? In the days of Grand Diplomacy he represented the sovereign, negotiated and made policy. Sir Stratford Canning did all these things a hundred years ago in Constantinople with grandeur. He made sure that he should not receive excessively rapid or precise instructions from London, by sending his despatches homeward by horseback through the Balkans. He performed very well too. Today no ambassador's representation of the Queen, negotiating ability or policy-making inclinations are of any importance. These men are required to represent today's Britain, to collect and report information, and to comment usefully on it as necessary. Our numerous political ministers will do the rest. Diplomats today are glorified journalists; and since a good many journalists are spryer and quicker on to both the news and its significance than they, it is permissible to wonder why they are so glorified. Mr Crossman, when Lord President of the Council, complained in a BBC programme suggestively called 'Change or Decay?' that Britain probably had the worst-informed government in the world, that decisions were often taken on desperately inadequate information as a result, and that far more experts were needed to leaven the civil servants. He cited the FO amongst other departments, and suggested that all too often the same officials were both sifting the intelligence and proposing the policy. This is true and can be dangerous, as some exploits of the CIA have shown. One elderly ambassador of mine suggested, jokingly, that diplomats should be heads of mission in their late twenties and thirties when the fire was still in them, with ambassadorial characters in their fifties on their staffs to proffer them sage advice. This may be going a bit far for our middle-aged Western civilisation, though ambassadors in their thirties and even late twenties come fairly often from the African and Asian states and do no worse than their elders. I can see Beatle George Harrison making a good ambassador, or High Commissioner as the old-fashioned title is, to India. He is highly presentable, original, energetic; he is a most successful businessman and dollar earner, as well as artist. He takes real trouble to penetrate the Indian mentality and art. He has a gorgeous wife. They are both gifted and good with people. (In fact the post has gone to a career diplomat.) One result of our system has been that considerable numbers of the brightest boys have quit in their thirties or early forties: Jock Colville, George Jellicoe, Viscount Norwich, Anthony Montague-Browne and Philip de Zulueta, to go no further. If the FO and Diplomatic Service cannot shed their esoteric and pompous image they will continue to get nowhere faster.

A final comment on the machinery. The Plowden committee was the best yet on what reforms were necessary, but that is not saying much. It at least included members from outside the interested Service; but they were all establishment types, many from Whitehall or thereabouts. Also it reported four years ago and the world moves fast. It is high time that the inadequacy of our diplomacy was investigated by a truly impartial body which might include, I suggest, an industrialist, a scientist, a journalist, a woman ('housewife'), a trade unionist, an academic, a management selection expert, a professional sportsman, an artist, and a public relations officer, one or more in his or her twenties or thirties, all of suitable calibre and none of them connected with Whitehall or Westminster. Their terms of reference should be wide and the emphasis should be on looking to the 1970s. They should at the same time investigate the Secret Intelligence Service. They would have to be shown top secrets as necessary. The officials would have to be under orders to collaborate fully and not to drag their feet. I have little doubt that the report would prove just as scathing as the Fulton report on the Home Civil Service.

The appointment in August 1968 of a small committee consisting of the industrialist Sir Val Duncan, the economist Andrew Shonfield, with the retired ambassador Sir Frank Roberts as ballast, for the purpose of a 'searching enquiry' into the working of our Diplomatic Service, is a step in the right direction. Its terms of reference, emphasising the importance of economic and commercial aptitude, are an advance on those given to the Plowden committee, as indeed they should be five years later. In fact they tally up to a point with my own ideas. But it remains to be seen how deeply this rather narrowly based committee is prepared to probe, and what proportion of their findings the FO mandarins are prepared to accept.

Of course the terms of reference of the committee I have suggested must not be in the void but must be relevant to the tasks to be done. Most important still, and in spite of widespread opposition arising from envy, ignorance and misunderstanding of the world facts of life, is to preserve and develop our good relationship with the US. This calls for new thinking and attitudes in our diplomacy. We have for too long taken the Americans for granted. Theirs is a complicated psychology and we have seldom put enough effort into studying it. At the same time we have arrogantly assumed that we do understand it instinctively. This has led to trouble and nasty surprises, and must be remedied. It is important in itself to have the most powerful nation in the world as a friend where our world-wide interests are concerned. It also affords us, always provided that we develop our own potentialities sufficiently to be for our part a useful friend to the US, a certain room for manœuvre, including outflanking, in dealing with difficult customers such as the French. We were able to play a useful auxiliary part in bringing about the important US-USSR non-proliferation treaty, since approved by a large majority in the UN. Typically, China, France, India and West Germany have not yet acceded, though East Germany has. Willy Brandt recently spoke with typical West German clumsiness to the assembled UN conference of non-nuclear countries. Renunciation of force was, he said, the indispensable criterion on which a security convention could be based; but he declined to say whether West Germany would renounce nuclear force.

Then the question of forming a North Atlantic Free Trade Area deserves more serious study than it has received. Some will protest that the links with the US will make our 'entry into Europe' impossible. First it is necessary to correct a good deal of loose thinking on this topic. 'Europe' is no more the EEC than it is the EFTA. It is both, plus the East European Comecon countries as well. That is the Europe at which we want to aim. The two strongest powers 'in Europe' are the US, located completely outside it, and the USSR which is half in Asia. As a matter of fact Britain is 'in Europe' on a large scale already: by way of private enterprise, in EFTA, in NATO and so on. Certainly we should continue to aim at membership of an expanded Common Market. But while we are stopped head on by de Gaulle we should be active in outflanking him so as to be in a stronger position when he is gone. The activation of 'the McDermott plan' would be a large step in the right direction, and it was encouraging that in 1967 Lord Chalfont, a highly capable Minister of State at the FO, gave something very much like it an airing to an international collection of journalists. This proved to be no more than a *ballon d'essai*, but it had the salutary effect of provoking shocked reactions by the French and West Germans. One useful result of recognising the GDR – which according to British diplomatic doctrine in no way implies approving of its government – would be that Western diplomats could be active in Ulbricht's hidebound country. We could also with advantage do more trade with the Comecon countries. Then it is good that George Brown, when Foreign Secretary, talked, even if ambiguously, of recognising the Oder-Neisse frontier for a start. So has Willy Brandt, now West Germany's Foreign Minister, while de Gaulle has come right out and recognised it. Also, while East Berlin is on the up and up, West Berlin is on the opposite trend. Its population is getting older and its young people more and more dissatisfied. The Western commandants and their large military and civilian staffs are archaic and powerless figures and the West Berliners would rather rule themselves, under the suitable safeguards I have proposed. My observation is that most West Germans sincerely want reunification, though a group of big industrialists have declared themselves against it. Probably most East Germans do too. But the unrealistic attitude of successive Bonn governments towards the GDR suggests that they do not want it badly enough; and certainly the GDR have no intention of making an unconditional surrender.

On 20th August 1968 the Red Army, supported by forces from Poland, Hungary, the GDR and Bulgaria, moved to occupy Czechoslovakia. It is still difficult to give a balanced estimate of future developments. The Soviet and Czechoslovak governments themselves cannot be altogether certain what is in store. The operation has caused both true revulsion and a great outburst of hypocrisy in the West and elsewhere. It has also betrayed the Soviet government's fears, not so much of triumphant 'liberalism' in Czechoslovakia or the USSR itself, but rather of exploitation by the very hard Maoists of any further weakening in the Soviet bloc.

Amongst the welter of tendentious comments it is worth trying to be objective. First, the operation was a short-term success for the invading Warsaw Pact powers. The forced, but frequent, description of it as a 'Soviet Bay of Pigs' is very wide of the mark. Secondly, the US government's shrewd and calm reaction, combined with its firm warning to the Soviet government to leave Romania and Jugoslavia alone, has admirably coped with the situation. Clearly the Soviet government were confident that no risk of war existed. In Chinese eyes this adds another great example of USSR-US collusion. Thirdly, Czechoslovakia previously had a government headed by the Communists Svoboda and Dubček and loyal to the Warsaw Pact; and she still has, Dubček handled matters with less skill than Ceauşescu in Romania and has been forced to backpedal. But in the broad political picture Czechoslovakia remains just where she was.

Beside the point is the sudden tender-heartedness for selected Communists, on the part of Western propagandists. This has embarrassed the Dubček government, given Moscow's propaganda a handle, and shown up the West's impotence. The third 'liberal' hero, Smrkovsky, is after all the man who declined General Patton's offer to liberate Prague in 1945 because he prefered to wait for the Red Army. The condemnation of all concerned by the Chinese has been equally impotent.

In the longer run Dubček will probably have his way, or most of it, and his allies' troops will go home (the GDR contingent have already done so). We must hope that the Soviet government's invitation to the American President to meet them, clumsily delivered to coincide with the occupation, will nevertheless be accepted in due course. In a wry way the affair has shown up once more both the USSR's fear of China and her dependence on US goodwill. I personally foresee not a revival of Stalinism in Eastern Europe, but rather a continued, if gradual,

trend towards liberalisation in the USSR and elsewhere.
For it remains as true as before the Czechoslovak operation that in Eastern Europe both politically and economically the monolith and the satellites have gone. If our diplomacy had recognised the process and exploited it with skill and in time, the Czechoslovak operation might even have been avoided; but the force of inertia in our diplomacy is an awesome thing. We should now cease referring to the iron curtain, which has been severely dented, and set our diplomacy to work wherever the opportunity may offer in Europe. This most decidedly includes sincere efforts to get closer relations with the USSR. The appointment of a powerful political figure as ambassador in Moscow, rather than the next official on the promotion list, might have helped here, but it has not come about. It would also help if we gave up thinking of the Russians even subconsciously as savages and laughing at their standard of living, and instead acknowledged less grudgingly their colossal achievements, power and potential influence for good in the world. What possible purpose can be served by Jeremy Thorpe, a man of no world importance, referring to the formerly great leader of the USSR, Khrushchev, as a drunken peasant? The negative attitude of many of our Kremlinologists who, usually from a safe billet in Fleet Street, expose and expound the alleged inner secrets of the Soviet government, are no great help here. Some so-called experts have written about the Czechoslovak crisis not merely with malignity towards the USSR but with scant attention to the facts. It is, for instance, considered acute to point out that some Soviet authority said one thing about Maoism in 1954 and a different thing in 1968. If only some of our political commentators, and diplomats, moved similarly with the times we should be better placed today. Again, Communist statements of fact or policy are disregarded at will, or simply denounced as false. This is altogether too *simpliste*. The majority of them are likely to be accurate and true, as the Communists are not congenital liars. Germany and Berlin constantly provide illustrations of

this fact. When the GDR government said that they would take stiff retaliatory measures if the quasi-Nazi emergency powers legislation was passed in Bonn, Kiesinger and Co treated their declarations as typical Communist bluff. They now know that they were not. It is Berlin again; and, if nothing is done, again and again. It is in fact wise to regard any story about Eastern Europe bearing the Bonn dateline as suspect; just as stories from Beirut about distant parts of the Arab world are as often as not fabrications, sometimes by the propaganda departments of the CIA or FO-cum-SIS. Some journalists are gullible; others, less to their credit, use such stories wittingly. The art in all this is to winnow the grain from the chaff. Our 'experts' tend to suffer from self-inflicted wounds, not least in falling a prey to believing their own propaganda.

However, a means is to hand for radically improving our relations with the East European states. This process can be conveniently handled through a complete reform of NATO when the organisation comes up for review in 1969. Having withdrawn our forces from their uselessly far-flung positions elsewhere we must on no account commit the *non sequitur* of increasing our military contribution to NATO. Characteristically, only Bonn has pressed for the strengthening of NATO in response to the occupation of Czechoslovakia. The other NATO nations, and in particular the US, have appreciated that it would be beside the point. George Kennan's view is that NATO was from the start 'unfortunate because it was quite unnecessary. . . . It was perfectly clear to anyone with even a rudimentary knowledge of the Russia of that day that the Soviet leaders had no intention of attempting to advance their cause by launching military attacks across frontiers.' That is a fair assessment, though Soviet expansionism in those days, which was basically defensive, had to be contained politically. Be that as it may, NATO as such is already of minor importance militarily: it is the US and the USSR who count in Europe as elsewhere. To quote only a few figures, the US will spend

£34,200 million this year on defence; Britain will spend about 1/16th of that. The US's per capita defence expenditure represents 9·2 per cent of the gross national product; Britain's is 6·4. But we cannot afford even this figure, which is well ahead of France's with 4·4 and almost double that of Germany with 3·6. This at a time when France's gold and foreign currency reserves, even after the losses resulting from last May, are just twice as large as ours and West Germany's four times as large. Relevant too, if in a different part of the world, is the fact that Japan's defence budget is one quarter the size of Britain's. NATO remains a very expensive toy in men and money. Not only should we not waste more of both, we should reduce our contribution by at least a half. There is no danger in this; and the plain fact is that if it comes to the crunch neither we nor our allies can effectively defend these islands. After that, but still it is to be hoped beginning in 1969, NATO can be deployed in a new and positive role: negotiation with the Warsaw Pact powers of a serious *détente* in Europe.

Next we must keep up the impetus in the United Nations. Lord Caradon has done great work here and we must never lapse back into our former standoffish and peevish attitude. The British sponsorship of the resolution for complete sanctions against Rhodesia is good diplomacy not only on the merits of the case but because it reassured our various African and Asian friends about the seriousness of our attitude on the question. In a connected sphere, it is good to see that the 1968 spring meeting of the executive council of the International Law Association included representatives not only of the obvious 'democracies' but of Czechoslovakia, Argentina, India and the USSR as well. This is a far cry from the attitude, still adopted by too many people, that such nations do not really understand the meaning of the word 'law'. On the Commonwealth we should shed our illusions. Australia and New Zealand are turning politically and economically towards the US, and good luck to them. We have contributed to the process by our weaknesses and by

224

sending to them a series of old-fashioned diplomats, including clapped-out major-generals masquerading as diplomats, as if to show that we do not take them seriously. The Commonwealth is worth preserving but it will never again be a great united force in the world. As with the UN so with the Commonwealth our attitude should be progressively more liberal and polycentric.

The entire *omnium gatherum* of backward-looking ideas has seldom been presented more comprehensively than by Patrick Wall, a right-wing Tory MP (and personal friend of mine) in a letter to the *Daily Telegraph*. It is headed 'British Resentments' and 'Truths Shown up by Powell Speech', referring to Enoch Powell's notorious 'racialist' speech of April 1968 in Birmingham. Now resentments are not a good basis for diplomacy; but Wall gives a long list of them. 'Our leaders are obsessed with internationalism. . . . The United Nations appear to rule our lives. . . . Our representatives abroad put first the appeasement of the government to whom they are accredited . . .' and so on. He states that 'trade follows the flag' which, given that the flag is no longer as far-flung as it was a generation ago, is fortunately not the case today. He goes on to say that 'a leader with a genuine programme of a return to patriotism and self-discipline could sweep the nation . . . a leader who would re-establish those principles that made us great.' The word leader – English for Führer – is used nine times in a short space. A couple of days later Wall was spat at by the students of Leeds University – he had criticised students' 'antics' in his letter – and his wife was called 'a Fascist pig', knocked down and trampled on. She described the episode as 'damn bad manners' and no one would quarrel with that. But it also showed, in a crude fashion, what a vast gulf is fixed between those who call for a return to our former greatness, which is impossible, and the young who have to cope with the world of the future. Wall also said that 'we resent being told that we are a fourth-class power'. Who tells us that? We are a power of the second rank, in a highly honourable position that can be preserved if we go about it the right way, but only on that condition. We resent, he added, having to borrow from the United States. In fact we have not only had to do so for forty years; we should be in a far worse position today if we were not able to do so. However, in a wry way Wall had the laugh on the others a few days later when a Gallup poll recorded an enormous majority in favour of Powellism – and of Powell as leader.

Wall also referred to our close ties with Rhodesia. Douglas-Home had recently been talking with Ian Smith, and it may or may not have been a coincidence that immediately afterwards our relations with Rhodesia took a decided turn for the worse. It is at least permissible to speculate that the opposition chief was not entirely loyal to Her Majesty's Government in all he said. One reputable newspaper went so far as to suggest that Douglas-Home might technically have been acting as a traitor to the Queen.

Similarly, when in May 1968 the first Russian warships to visit the Persian Gulf since the revolution paid their courtesy calls, there was a minor panic in some British quarters. Douglas-Home thought it right to exploit the news to criticise the British government in a speech made abroad, and stated that Europe's oil supplies must be secured against the increasing Soviet influence in the Middle East. Who was he to speak for Europe? He was in no position to speak even for Britain. Why should he assume that the Soviet government wished to tamper with Middle Eastern oil supplies? And how would he suggest that we 'secure' them – by sending a gunboat? In all too many minds the futile hankering after the gunboat diplomacy of the Victorian era lives on. There is no reason why the expansion of Soviet influence in the Middle East should not have a calming effect in the long run. Our diplomats should be instructed to get on good terms with those Soviet officials and bodies responsible for the new trend and to help them where they usefully can with ideas and the lessons of our experience. Much more to the point then all this woolly thinking in fairly high places is the news, published on the same day, that Guest, Keen & Nettlefolds are making a strong bid for the newly developing Russian car service station market which could be worth millions of pounds and which will impinge on millions of Soviet citizens. That constitutes a useful piece of diplomacy, as well as good business.

The British Press is not always a help where our diplomacy is concerned. We have now as good a collection of foreign reporters as any press in the world: we have caught up on the Americans in this sphere over the past twenty years. But when it comes to the interpretation of the news we are less well provided. The balance is fairly kept in Lord Thomson's *Times* newspapers, the *Mirror* group, and up to a point in David Astor's *Observer*. But elsewhere anything goes. Big words like 'patriotism' are worked to death. It is as well to remember the wise Dr Johnson's dictum: patriotism, sir, is the last refuge of the scoundrel. There can never have been a keener example than that of the egregious Jordanian Sirhan Sirhan, who as he shot Robert Kennedy dead cried: 'I do it for my country. I love my country.' He had not been near his country, if Jordan can be called that, for years. The immediate comment by Dr Mohammad Mehdi, the secretary-general of the action committee on US-Arab relations, was charming too: 'We condemn the fact that Senator Kennedy kowtowed to Zionism, just as we condemn the action of Mr Sirhan.' Today Dr Johnson would have extended that judgment to 'nationalism', which we use pejoratively to mean patriotism on the part of any people other than your own. When Philby was asked recently in Moscow how he felt about being a traitor all his life he replied: 'Traitor, traitor to what? I was faithful to my beliefs throughout.'

Then how often do we read in the right-fringe Press, which is a large proportion of the whole, of some marvellous British trade coup, aircraft construction or other achievement which is on the point of coming off but – owing to bad luck, of course, or unsporting foreigners – just does not. Or again, as a supreme young US athlete remarked, this part of the Press seems content with very little: 'British runner's magnificent achievement. Comes seventeenth in tough international field.' Fortunately however, although we are probably the most assiduous readers of the Press in the world, the large majority of us are far from accepting all its words as gospel.

Withdrawal symptoms are always painful; but when the withdrawal is over the patient is better than before. We have overstretched and misdirected our resources for so long that the remedy seems unpleasant to some people, particularly that considerable section which lives nostalgically in the past. It is in the past that much of our diplomacy lives and operates. The trouble there is that we may delude ourselves that we are doing fine; but we shall not delude anyone else, from the US to Nauru. Emotive terms such as 'little Englander' or 'a second Sweden' miss the point. Not that there is much wrong with being a Swede. Amongst the twenty-one nations who are members of the Organisation for Economic Co-operation and Development the per capita gross national product is of course greatest in the US; Sweden comes second and we rank seventh equal with Belgium. We not only could but must do better. Our economy is still potentially one of the strongest in the world and our inventiveness first class; it is a question of trading intensively and universally if we are to keep going at all. The more we can transfer totally unproductive expenditure and manpower from our unnecessarily large forces – which are nevertheless laughable to those in the big league – to the industrial production that is essential to us, the better. A total defence expenditure of say a thousand million pounds per annum, approximately half the present sum, should be adequate. This can be attained by pushing further the integration already achieved by Healey at the Ministry of Defence and integrating the three services into one Royal Defence Force. Then we can contribute perhaps as much as an open-handed one per cent of our gross national product – or twice as much as at present – in aid to emerging countries to whom we richly owe it and, incidentally, as a sweetener to our diplomacy. Not that we should expect too much gratitude; we have done too well out of our colonies in the past, and put too little into them, for that. But judicious aid will help to even up our position compared with that of the Communist powers, who have no colonial past and no racialism. Then our traders and diplomats will be able to look people in the eye all over the world and not feel that they are being laughed at behind their backs. Then we can, with the help of forward-looking diplomacy, make our proper weight, which is very considerable, felt in the world while avoiding the collisions and shocks which are bound to occur if we walk along looking backwards. That proper weight will be much appreciated in the future line-up of powers: the US, the USSR, ourselves and Japan, in the crucial test against thermonuclear China.

All this seems, and is, a far cry from the Eden epoch and style. In the dozen years since he retired the face of the world has changed radically. The tempo of diplomacy has become even more hectic, and this process will continue. Nevertheless it is, I think, fair to attribute to the Eden legacy some of the shortcomings in our diplomacy in these last years. In part they are due to his personal colleagues, both political and official, who still carry on in the polite, tidy, euphoric manner which was considered *de rigueur* under his dispensation. Only last year a recently retired ambassador could write a book on diplomatic method wholly in the Eden style, and recommending amongst other things that every young diplomat should get off to a slow start by reading Harold Nicolson on the subject. Che Guevara's works would be more to the point.

Of course it is not all Eden's fault. It is the fault of us all in Britain. Specifically it is the fault of all those connected with diplomacy who go along today in a style which has been out of touch with reality for a generation. Eden and the Prince of Wales, the golden boys of the 1920s and 1930s, are over seventy now. They hav had, and still have as Avon and Windsor, luxurious, full and influential lives.

They are not tragic figures, but pathetic: British aristocrats totally at a loss in the world of the sixties where almost no one, even in his own country, has time for their style and attitudes. Occasionally Eden still takes upon himself to make a political pronouncement. He has taken the US government to task more than once over Vietnam, and he regularly harks back fourteen years to his 'great' year of 1954. This does not endear him to the US authorities who never found him lovable even then. And his efforts have been politely but firmly rejected by the Soviet side too. Thus the Eden style continues, full of those good intentions with which hell is paved, but off the beam. I wonder whether, looking around at the shambles in the Middle East and elsewhere, and at Britain's poor posture in the thick of it, the thought ever crosses his mind: *Si monumentum requiris, circumspice*? I should doubt it.

It is not quite too late to stop the rot provided we draw and apply thoroughly the lessons of the decline of British diplomacy and of Britain's position in the world. But lively actions and reactions are essential, and the creation of a better-than-contemporary style. Who wears an Anthony Eden hat today? Only Mr Steptoe, Mr Enoch Powell and, rather curiously, Mr Kosygin. And, of course, all those Carleton-Browne characters at the FO.

Bibliography

Avon, Earl of (Anthony Eden), *Memoirs*, 3 vols, Cassell, 1960–5

Ball, George W, *The Discipline of Power*, The Bodley Head, 1968

Bromberger, Merry and Serge, *Secrets of Suez*, translated, Sidgwick and Jackson, 1957

Campbell-Johnson, Alan, *Sir Anthony Eden*, Robert Hale, 1955

Carr, E H, *What is History?* Pelican, 1961

Chandos, Viscount, *Memoirs*, The Bodley Head, 1962

Churchill, Randolph, *The Rise and Fall of Sir Anthony Eden*, MacGibbon and Kee, 1959
With Winston S Churchill Jr, *The Six Day War*, Heinemann, 1967

Churchill, Winston S, *The Second World War*, 6 vols, Cassell, 1948–54

Colvin, Ian, *Vansittart in Office*, Gollancz, 1965

Cooper, Duff, *Old Men Forget*, Rupert Hart-Davis, 1953

Dulles, Allen, *The Craft of Intelligence*, Weidenfeld and Nicolson, 1963

Foreign Office List and Diplomatic and Consular Year Book, The, Harrison and Sons, 1865–1965. Since then, *The Diplomatic Service List*, HMSO

Fulbright, Senator J William, *The Arrogance of Power*, Jonathan Cape, 1967

Hayter, Sir William, *The Kremlin and the Embassy*, Hodder and Stoughton, 1966

Hitler, Adolf, *Mein Kampf*, 1929

Kahn, Herman, *On Thermonuclear War*, Weidenfeld and Nicolson, 1960
Thinking about the Unthinkable, Weidenfeld and Nicolson, 1962
On Escalation, Pall Mall Press, 1965

Kennan, George F, *American Diplomacy 1900–50*, Secker and Warburg, 1951
Russia and the West under Lenin and Stalin, Hutchinson, 1961
Memoirs, Hutchinson, 1968

Macmillan, Harold, *The Blast of War*, Macmillan, 1967

McNamara, Robert S, *The Essence of Security*, Hodder and Stoughton, 1968

Moncrieff, Anthony, ed, *Suez Ten Years After*, BBC, 1967

Moran, Lord, *Winston Churchill, The Struggle for Survival*, Constable, 1966

Mowat, Charles Loch, *Britain between the Wars 1918–1940*, Methuen, 1955

Mowat, R C, *Middle East Perspective*, Blandford Press, 1958

Murphy, G A, *Egypt's Liberation: The Philosophy of the Egyptian Revolution*, Public Affairs Press, Washington, 1955

Nicolson, Harold, *Diplomacy*, OUP, 1942
The Evolution of the Diplomatic Method, Constable, 1954
Diaries and Letters, Collins, 1966–8

Northedge, F S, *British Foreign Policy 1945–61*, Allen and Unwin, 1962

Nutting, Anthony, *No End of a Lesson*, Constable, 1967

Page, Bruce; Leitch, David; Knightley, Philip, *Philby*, André Deutsch, 1968

Pelling, Henry, *Modern Britain 1885–1955*, Nelson, 1960

Plowden, Lord, chairman, *Report of the Committee on Representational Services Overseas*, HMSO, 1964

Sampson, Anthony, *Anatomy of Britain*, Hodder and Stoughton, 1962

Seton-Watson, H, *Neither War nor Peace*, Methuen, 1960

Strang, Lord, *The Foreign Office*, Allen and Unwin, 1955
Home and Abroad, André Deutsch, 1956
Britain in World Affairs, Faber & Faber, 1961
The Diplomatic Career, André Deutsch, 1962

Taylor, A J P, *English History 1914–1945*, OUP, 1965

Thayer, Charles, *Diplomat*, Michael Joseph, 1960

Thomas, Hugh, *The Suez Affair*, Weidenfeld and Nicolson, 1967

Truman, Harry S, *Year of Decisions, 1945*, Hodder & Stoughton, 1955

Ulbricht, Walter, *Whither Germany?* Zeit im Bild Publishing House, Dresden, 1967

Wilmot, Chester, *The Struggle for Europe*, Collins, 1952

Index